LETTER
IN A
WOODPILE

LETTER
IN A
WOODPILE

Essays from
NPR's *All Things Considered*
Commentator

ED CULLEN

COOL SPRINGS PRESS
A Division of Thomas Nelson Publishers
Since 1798

Dedication

For Martha Lynn

Published by Cool Springs Press
a Division of Thomas Nelson, Inc.,
P. O. Box 141000
Nashville, Tennessee, 37214

Cataloging in Publication information is available.
ISBN: 1591862493

First printing 2006
Printed in the United States of America
10 9 8 7 6 5 4 3 2 1

Cover Design by Bruce Gore, Gore Studios
Typesetting by S.E. Anderson

Cool Springs Press books may be purchased in bulk
for educational, business, fundraising, or sales
promotional use. For information, please email
SpecialMarkets@ThomasNelson.com.

Visit the Thomas Nelson website at
www.ThomasNelson.com and the Cool Springs Press
website at **www.coolspringspress.net**

Contents

Foreword, 11

My Father's Kite, 15
Generation Shift, 17
The Boar, 19
Fishing with Meredith, 22
The Manta Ray, 24
Tutti Frutti Girl, 27
New Orleans, the Poem, 29
Bobby's Marbles, 31
Night Passage, 34
Prom Night, 37
Truck Repair, a Revelation, 39
Leaf Blowing, 42
Welcome to the Pack, 45
Fishing with Malcolm, 47
The Heart Volcano, 50
Letter in a Woodpile, 53
Block That Stress!, 56
Tiger Charge, 59
For Cat's Sake, 61
Aroma Inventory, 64

Home Schooling, 66
Flip-flops, 68
The Elgin, 70
The Hurricane Game, 72
The Necessity of Repetition, 75
Learning from a New Teacher, 77
The Attic Fan, 80
Around Midnight, 82
Porch Steps Baseball, 84
Hale-Bopp, 86
Phoning Harry, 89
October Best, 92
First Fire, 94
Velvet Purple Coronet Wind Thing, 97
The Best Game I Never (Really) Played, 99
Romancing the Nose, 102
Hamsters, 104
Who Is What They Used to Be, 107
Driver's Ed, 110
Bobby's Gun, 112
Amal Is Back, 115
Thunder Happy, 117
Those High Flying Tree Guys, 120
Winter Cyclists, 123
Convenience Stores Offer Look at Culture, 125
The Visitor, 127
Cat People, 129
Chilling During Surgery, 131
Christmas Calling, 134

Foreword

My first venture into publishing was on a borrowed typewriter. I was ten years old. The result was a one-page newspaper with stories about new neighbors and the births of dogs, cats, and children. We had crime stories which were vague because the suspects worked on the newspaper.

With the help of carbon paper, the no-name newspaper had a press run of ten copies on a good day. Then, according to my mother, I put on my oldest, most patched clothes to sell the papers door to door. It was my first lesson in marketing and playing to an audience.

I'm fifty-nine as this collection of essays goes to press. The essays were broadcast on National Public Radio's "All Things Considered" or published in *The Sunday Advocate* (Baton Rouge) in slightly different form. This collection came about after a book publicist heard me on her radio in Connecticut. My career, already moving at glacial speed, inched ahead.

Though fifty years have passed since my first attempt at journalism, the reason I write hasn't changed. I can't NOT write, especially while wearing old clothes.

—Ed Cullen

Does anticipation diminish
with age or only the
belief that anticipation will
amount to anything?

My Father's Kite

One spring Sunday afternoon when I was in grammar school, my father tried to hit the ionosphere with a box kite.

After working for hours at the dining room table, he finished making a kite the old way, the *only* way to his thinking, with paste made of water and flour, sheets of newspaper, and split bamboo sticks.

"Grab your jacket," he said, rising from the table with the kite held gingerly in one big hand.

We drove to the schoolyard as quiet as pallbearers.

Arriving at the deserted school, my father jumped out of the car with the kite and trotted onto a field of stomped dirt and thin grass. I followed with a ball of twine half the size of my head.

My father tossed the construction of wooden sticks and newspaper into a stiff breeze. He tugged expertly at the kite's string, each jerk of his wrist sending the kite higher. Our first spool of twine burned itself to the stick handle in no time.

Dad had tied together three balls of twine when he began yelling, "More string! We need more string!" He might as well have been on the Russian steppes crying for buttermilk. Where was I supposed to get kite string?

My father handed me the ball of string and stick, dived into our car, and sped away.

I stood alone in the familiar schoolyard feeling like the last boy on earth. The kite was so high in the late afternoon sky that it wasn't even a full speck. I held onto the stick of wood, letting my eyes follow the giant bend of string skyward. We'd sent a message to the kite by cutting a slot in a piece of Big Chief tablet paper and slipping the paper onto the string. The wind carried the piece of paper up, up, up.

I imagined a man in a passing airliner looking through a round, curtained window. "Look, Ethel," the man said, "that kite is about to receive a message."

I stood in the wind as hundreds of yards of twine tried to pull my arm free of its socket.

My father returned with an armload of balled kite string. The light drained from the sky. The kite ate string and demanded more. I knew my father wouldn't quit without help, so I said, "Dad, can we go home, now?"

My father pulled and wrapped kite string around the stick until his fingers bled. Then, he cut the string with his pocketknife, and we got into the car. The kite we hadn't seen in hours was never seen again—by us.

"Tomorrow, you can tell your classmates that your kite flew a mile over the school," my father said.

We may have released a mile of kite string over L.S. Rugg Grammar School, but no one was going to hear about it from me. My father talked about "writing up a little story for the newspaper," but, mercifully, his mind skated on to other things.

A week later, I was riding my bicycle past the schoolyard when I saw a man and a boy standing in the middle of the playground. I let my eyes follow their skyward gazes to a yellow kite dancing in a blue-white sky. I pedaled on, free of the twine that binds.

16

Generation Shift

It delights junior colleagues to discover what people my age call "Three on the Tree," first, second, and third gears on the steering column. Driving to lunch one day, a young reporter leaned over to see what I was doing with my left foot. I was depressing the clutch, of course, to move through the gears of an almost twenty-five-year-old pickup truck.

It turns out—or so I'm told by people in their twenties—that car and truck makers stopped putting manual shift levers on the steering column years ago.

Now, pickup trucks with manual transmissions have their shifters between driver and passenger, a stupid place to put a shifter if you ask me. That space is reserved for power tools and large dogs.

Gone are the cigar lighter and the ashtray. I smoke an occasional cigar, so I like a fire option when fishing, as well as an electrical outlet. I keep change, also screws, nuts, and bolts in the ashtray, a spacious drop-down compartment the size of a horse's jaw.

Holding on to cars and pickup trucks for ten to twenty years, as I do, my rides tend to be a little out of date.

"What's this?" a luncheon companion asked as he unlocked and pushed open one of the triangular vent windows of my antique truck.

"It directs air across the inside of the cab," I said, while depressing the clutch to go from first to third. My passenger didn't notice the first to third trick we on-the-column manual shifters like to do to break the monotony of driving.

"Cool," my twenty-something colleague said. He'd just found the large tabs for pre-setting stations on the truck's non-digital radio. "My grandfather's car had a radio like this."

My truck and passengers are about the same age. I've tried, half-heartedly, to sell the truck, but no one who's looked at it wants a truck that shifts on the column. Shifts period, for that matter.

A cop told me manual-shift cars and trucks are stolen less frequently than ones with automatic transmission. A lot of car thieves are the same ages as my kid colleagues.

This morning, I was filling my fountain pen when a woman in her twenties walked by my desk.

"What *is* that?" she asked.

"Manual transmission ballpoint," I said, as I dipped the fountain pen's nib into the little bottle of . . . oh, never mind.

The Boar

We used to arrive at the Tree Farm late on Friday. In winter, there was enough light to see to the first bend in the road. Overgrown in summer with brambles that snatched at clothing and tore the skin, the road was burned black in winter and no threat to flesh.

The gate fell away in the truck's headlights as I slipped the heavy links of chain and pushed. There was a creak of hinges and a soft crash as the gate stopped in tall brush. My father-in-law once described the Tree Farm's gate as the barrier between what he had to do to make a living and his life as keeper of guinea hens and goats.

He'd grown up on land my wife and her family call The Farm. He owned the place with brothers and sisters. The Tree Farm was his alone. A council made decisions at The Farm. A sovereign who worked in a suit that he'd once worn to the office ruled the Tree Farm.

My father-in-law built a barn, chicken houses, a pen for hogs, and started on a board-and-batten house before he died. The wood had come from the place, milled into stout pine boards at a sawmill up the road. We'd helped in small ways, but it was his place. Months went by after his death before anyone felt like driving three hours to work on the house.

Arriving at nightfall, we'd spend the hours before bedtime setting up camp inside the unfinished cabin. After a Saturday morning breakfast, my wife, brother-in-law and I would go to work. My son and daughter were free to roam as long as they stayed in "Hoo-ing" distance.

My son was a confident four-year-old the morning he stepped into the barn crib. When he screamed, I ran to the sound, imagining him fallen from the loft or backed against boards by a snake. I saw every bad thing that can happen to a child when a parent gets himself out of position. I stopped in the opening to the crib, peering past my son to a boar's skull, hair clinging to bone, face fixed in the fierce smile of the dead.

We didn't know if the boar had been left behind when the other animals were rounded up or if he'd come to this empty place from another farm. My son had no fear of the barn once he understood that the boar's hair and bones were but another feature of the Tree Farm, like his grandfather's suit coat hanging from a fence post.

Now, it's my son who goes to the two farms most often. He drives alone or with friends. He stops for gasoline and ice, fingering welder's caps and do-rags he has no intention of buying. I make the drive with him sometimes, fiddling with the radio to find a ball game while following at a safe distance in driving rain the flooded taillights of an old pickup truck.

In the winter, I see him opening the gate to the treacherous track through the woods. His truck's tires grip patches of old sand and gravel then slide onto slick, gray mud. He twists the steering wheel, heart hammering, foot playing clutch, gas pedal, and brakes like an organist. He makes the last turn, and he's at the little house. The adrenaline drains off as he carries groceries, sleeping bag, and ice chest inside.

Years ago, I could walk the quarter mile from the house to the highway without a flashlight. I navigated by whatever light there was in the night sky and the tree tops along the sand and gravel track. Timber harvests, storms, and pine beetles have changed the landscape. I need new navigational guides.

I think, sometimes, I need to spend more time at the Tree Farm with my son. But I would try to make him see it as I first saw it. He must see it his own way. Like the story of the boar, I have my version. He has his.

Fishing with Meredith

Fishing with a woman is the same as fishing with a guy—but different.

Meredith, who lives down the street and occasionally takes me fishing, combs her hair and puts on makeup before grabbing up her rods and reels. The makeup isn't for me. Meredith gussies up to go to the grocery store.

So, I comb *my* hair, bathe, and put on clean shirt and jeans. These are preparations men don't make when fishing with other men. Men don't bathe before fishing because they say the smell of soap alerts nature to their presence. So does banging paddles on the sides of boats, but modern man needs a reason not to bathe.

I have never caught a fish with Meredith, and I'm not a bad fisherman, either.

"Oh, this pond is hard to fish," Meredith will say, reeling in a bass or a hefty sac-a-lait.

Meredith sometimes catches the same fish over and over—or thinks she does.

"Oh, look, it's my fish," she says.

You half expect the bass she's just boated to rub against her leg and give her a big wet one right on the lips.

Men don't say things like that. If we caught the same bass cast after cast we'd say, "Oh, yeah, that's five. They're biting today, ol' buddy."

Television fishing shows have taught men how to talk while on the water.

"Whoa, Nelly, another big one. Come to poppa, big 'un."

When Meredith hooks a big one, she gets very quiet and concentrates on what she's doing until the bass is in the boat. Oh, sure she catches fish. Anyone can catch fish if he concentrates.

Meredith and I are at the age when line snarled at the rod tip is hard to see.

"Darn, is my line wrapped around the tip of the rod?" Meredith asks.

There are women who curse as fluently as men. Not Meredith. After I've been in her company for a few hours, my own expletives lose their fire.

"Gosh darn it all to heck, anyway."

That is an exact Meredith quote after she hooked a log three casts in a row.

When I fish with Meredith, it's always on the same pond, a lovely, hidden, saucer of whiskey brown water in an old subdivision. The pond's owners live in houses with wooden decks overlooking the water. A friend of Meredith's, a woman who doesn't fish, lives in one of the houses.

The two women stand on the bank visiting while I take a canoe and begin to work the lily pads, half-sunken logs, and dark spots of water under low-hanging willow branches. Meredith is polite. She wants to be in the boat with me, flipping lures, but one simply does not turn one's back on one's hostess.

I love fishing with Meredith. It's so civilized.

The Manta Ray

People in my hometown bemoan the loss of a former opera house most of them knew as the Paramount Theater.

I saw mush movies with my mother at the Paramount, memorizing the ornate detail of the ceiling during kissing scenes. I saw my first Dracula movie at the Paramount. The theater's blood-red, crushed velvet curtains parted to a collective intake of breath. My next conscious breath came when the house lights came up. I sat through the movie a second time to see what it looked like without fingers spread before my face.

If a movie failed to hold my attention past the first showing, I spent a little time exploring the building. There were subterranean bathrooms, a balcony, and elevated box seats.

The box seats jutted from the wall a story above the floor. You entered them through archways after climbing an enclosed stair. There were red draperies in the archways. It was a grand feeling to push aside the heavy curtains, but children were banned from the box seats. If they made it into an unoccupied box, they sat scooched down to avoid detection by the floor usher on the other side of the theater. It helped if the usher who guarded the stairs was on a smoke break.

My mother refused to sit in the box seats and ordered me to stay out, and it wasn't because couples sat there to smooch. My mother was certain the box seats were going to part company with the walls. The roof of the Paramount collapsed years later, long after my mother had died. I wish I had some way to get word to her.

She heard about the jacket incident, though. The way my father's voiced carried, the whole town heard about it.

My father had taken me to the Paramount one afternoon. I remember it all quite clearly. I was supposed to be in the restroom or at the popcorn counter, but I was exploring. I wasn't in one of the box seats more than a few minutes before I realized the movie was just as boring high up as it was at floor level. I peered down into the darkened theater. Just then, light from the screen revealed that I was directly over my father's pale, bald head. He was looking straight ahead, as one would expect a father to do at the picture show.

I slipped out of my Eisenhower jacket, a short, itchy coat that gripped the wearer at the waist and poofed out front, sides, and back. Who knows what my lizard brain was thinking, but I held the jacket at arm's length before letting go.

The jacket fell for about an hour, blossoming like a night flower, fanning out to the shape of a manta ray to envelope my father's eared dome. He could not have imagined what had taken possession of his head, but when his heart resumed pumping blood to his brain he figured it out.

As in my Dracula blackout, I lost conscious thought for the time it took to flee the box seat, tumble down the carpeted stairway, and dash down marble steps into the tiled, subterranean men's bathroom. I remember hearing a snatch of movie dialog when the door opened. My father was holding the Eisenhower jacket in one clinched hand. He wasn't smiling.

I don't remember the spanking, but I know it was a good one. I remember nothing about the movie, but I feel right now my father's disappointment. There are things my father and I never got to talk about. I'd like to hear his version of that afternoon.

For as long as I saw movies in the Paramount Theater, no matter how good the movie, no matter how special the girl I was with, my eyes would search out that box seat to watch for a ghostly manta ray falling onto a bald man's head.

*

Tutti Frutti Girl

In that deepest part of summer when the seasonal pendulum pauses before starting to swing toward fall, I see the mystery girl over her tutti frutti snow cone and behind her Mrs. Bordelon parking her limousine in front of the A&P.

I was fourteen, working inside a gaudy snow ball stand cooled by an overworked window air conditioner. The highlight of each long afternoon was feeding a fresh block of frozen water into the whirling knives of a machine to make shaved ice.

The snow ball stand rested on two tires and a Coke crate on a molten asphalt lot across the street from the A&P. I came to know well the grocery store's customers, especially Mrs. Bordelon, a woman I recognized from my Aunt Aggie's canasta games. A tiny woman in her seventies, Mrs. Bordelon drove a long, black Cadillac limousine to the A&P two or three times a day. Each docking at the curb required at least five minutes.

I watched the shadow of the A&P shorten, then lengthen, as I waited for the early afternoon rush of small children and their dogs. There was a girl, who may have been visiting someone in the neighborhood, who came to the stand for two weeks. I would watch her approach, fresh print blouse over shorts, feet in white Ked's tennis shoes.

As the last of summer inched toward leather shoes, new blue jeans, and the routine of school, my days facing tall skinny bottles filled with red, green, purple, and yellow syrup slowed to a crawl. When the girl approached, slow motion and fast forward fused into no time.

She placed her order and I filled it—tutti frutti. As I handed her the cone, her face seemed large and looming over the curvature of the snow cone. My cold fingers brushed her warm fingers. She slipped the quarter through the slot under the screened window and began her slow walk back up the block.

Forty years later, that girl visits my memories, her face half obscured by a hill of ice while, behind her, an old woman visits the A&P now for eggs, now for lettuce, now for avocados.

New Orleans, the Poem

Visiting our friend Joellen on South Tonti Street, I see the New Orleans that the tourists miss.

Below her kitchen window, green parrots, wings edged in blue, compete with pigeons, cardinals and house wrens for seed in a bird feeder. The wild parrots of New Orleans, descendants of escaped pets, thrive in the semi-tropical climate.

A thunderstorm is gathering over St. Rita's Catholic Church on Upperline a few blocks away. The congregation of elderly parishioners is saying goodbye to the cantor, a young man who sings the "Ave Maria" as though he wrote it.

On Magazine Street, young people in fashionably funky clothes sit at tables outside coffee shops, keeping dogs company as 6:15 p.m. becomes 6:16.

A tall man walks by with a Rottweiler at his heel and a tame parrot on his shoulder. Down the sidewalk go man, bird, and dog, past antique shops where garden trowels that once did honest work wear $60 price tags.

At Domilise's restaurant, a few blocks off Jefferson, a woman behind the counter looks up to see a familiar face about to place a lunch order.

"Get back here and make it yourself, dahlin,'" the counter woman yells.

"Once she gets to know you, you don't get no royal treatment," another sandwich maker cackles.

Around two o'clock, a thunderstorm rolls up the sky, smelling of slate roofs and the Mississippi River. Rain falls as though poured from a bucket onto people and parrots. Pedestrians make careful haste over sidewalks raised by the roots of hundred-year-old live oak trees.

Old women on slanting, wooden porches, women whose mothers wore white gloves to shop on Canal Street as late as the 1960s, use the backs of their legs to scoot iron, shell-shaped chairs out of the reach of the rain. Safe from the deluge, the women reseat themselves. They use fingertips to pull back wisps of hair from faces that say, "Where were we?"

Bobby's Marbles

The gift of a bag of marbles from my cousin Bobby would end up one of the biggest burdens of my childhood.

I loved Bobby. He was fifteen years older than I. He towered over me, his round friendly face looking down to tell me how to tie a knot or hold a baseball. A souvenir tomahawk hung by a leather strap from the doorknob of his bedroom. In time, I would inherit that art object and hang it from the doorknob of *my* bedroom door. Hanging there, the tomahawk, unlike the bag of marbles, was a talisman against outside threat.

My cousin's room might have inspired an illustration in *Boy's Life* magazine. A sturdy single bed stood in one corner and next to it a desk with lamp where one might do homework or sit to dream. The room's windows overlooked the yard. The smells that floated past billowing curtains changed with the seasons. The sounds of cars, their drivers shifting through the gears, clutching, braking, accelerating, came through the open windows with the smells of earth and flowers. Blue jays and squirrels insulted one another in the high branches of a pecan tree. It all smelled and sounded right.

But back to the tomahawk. Some western river had polished a big oval stone to the smoothness of a still pond. A human—probably not an Indian—had split a sawed-off tree sapling, slipped the stone between the cleaved branch, and bound all tightly with a long strip of rawhide.

Then, in what could only have been divine inspiration, the ax maker painted the ends of the rock blood red. Thus configured, rock and sapling made a stone ax an Indian warrior might have fashioned at Boy Scout camp.

Anything Bobby did was admirable. I just wished he'd chosen another cousin to present his moldy canvas sack and its dreadful weight of marbles. I wasn't such a clod that I couldn't appreciate the treasure inside that smelly bag. The marbles were beautiful—taws, crystals, aggies, cat's eyes, steelies. If only I had been given permission to hoard the marbles to examine in good light with a jeweler's loop over a glass of cognac in my old age.

But no. My cousin handed me the bag with the understanding that I would be as good at marbles as he. Bobby was sure that I would pass down twice as many marbles to a cousin then drooling into his bib.

The muscles in my stomach tightened as an opponent drew a circle in the dirt and threw down his marbles. I selected some of the less desirable marbles from Bobby's bag and kissed them good-bye. It would have been quicker and less painful to have just given the challenger a handful of marbles.

I had no strength in my fingers, no steely snap of forefinger and thumb. My shots barely made it across the line scratched into the dirt. In the hands of an expert, the "shooter" flew from a side-turned fist, arrived at the target faster than the eye could follow, and sent the resting marble out of the circle with a *click*! One second, I was looking at the target marble. The next, I was regarding with awe the "shooter" spinning, sizzling in the first marble's place.

My "shooter" didn't fly. It fell from my cocked fingers, rolled listlessly a few inches and quit. The opponent's marbles couldn't have been safer if they'd been down at Guarantee Bank in a safety deposit box. "Losers," "keepers," "shooters," they were all the same to me. Marbles in my custody quickly passed into other hands. My cousin's sack of marbles grew ever lighter.

"That sack of marbles must be getting pretty heavy," Bobby would say, and I'd mumble words that would have been a lie if they'd been audible.

When we studied the stock market crash of '29 in American history class, I knew why those poor men had jumped from the windows of tall buildings. They had tried in vain to enhance their marble holdings. Down to their last marble, they'd gambled, lost, walked to the window, and stepped out.

The day I lost the last of Bobby's marbles, I sang. I skipped home, hugged my mother, and started on homework without being told.

Night Passage

Driving through the night in a twenty-year-old pickup truck, windows down, wrapped in darkness, headlights illuminating a long, conical world, I quickly reach a sense of no time.

I'm driving the I-10 across the Atchafalaya Basin. The elevated road across America's largest swamp wilderness makes speedboats of cars, mighty ships of eighteen-wheelers.

Leaving Lafayette as dusk becomes night, I'm eastbound, heading for Baton Rouge. Before me stretches a double line of red taillights. The lights float in the night like a lava flow.

The night is so right, air cool, sky full of stars, that it is good to be driving alone, no tape in the machine, listening instead through an open window to an opera sung by frogs and crickets. I'll switch the radio on in a few minutes to catch the last of the Astros game on the final approach to Baton Rouge.

A man I know swears that a flying saucer flew beside his car one night crossing the Atchafalaya Basin. The saucer, he said, flew just on the other side of the railing as car and spaceship flew over the great swamp. I never know what to say to people who insist they've seen flying saucers. So, I said, "Really?"

Yes, a flying saucer had hung just over the railing of the elevated highway, mere feet from the side of the man's car.

"For how long?" I asked.

"Miles," the man said.

I let it go at that. But I have often wondered if a flying saucer would make the drive across the basin at night any more interesting. Only more distracting, I've decided.

I'm not saying I wouldn't mind looking over Whiskey Bay to see a flying saucer flitting through the cypress trees, flying low over the water to pull up suddenly beside my truck. I'm not saying I wouldn't be thrilled to glance at the saucer to see the silhouette of a fellow driver. I'm saying I don't think it would add that much to my enjoyment of a basin crossing at night.

I'd driven to Lafayette to see my son. The drive over was good until I got the unmistakable whiff of boiling radiator as I hit the city limits. I made it to my son's house and called a tow truck. Two nights later, I was heading back to Baton Rouge.

A failed water pump means you have to build confidence anew in an old truck. It may be cheaper to keep an old pickup running than it is to buy a new one, but you pay a price at every new engine noise as you cross the Atchafalaya Basin at night.

For drivers with cell phones, the emergency telephones attached to poles on the I-10 swamp expressway must seem quaint. Drive an old truck and the telephone boxes remind you of the age of every component under the hood. At the first Baton Rouge sign, my confidence in the truck soared.

I breathed deeply, testing the air for trouble, but I smelled only damp night air, cooling concrete, and hot rubber. At the last Baton Rouge sign before the

Mississippi River Bridge, I switched the radio back on to hear the box scores of an Astros win. Then, I turned the radio low to listen to the truck's smooth power as I drove the last minutes of a night passage over the basin.

Prom Night

I see a high school couple in a restaurant on prom night and fall into a time tunnel that drops me into the spring of 1964.

It's early evening inside a brick veneer house where my date's father circles with a 35mm camera, like a hunter looking for an open shot at caribou.

"Come on, you two! Smile! Come on. Big Smile!"

Already grinning like a death's head, I stretch my lips into thin lines that meet at the back of my head. Finally, my date cries, "Da-DEE!" and our torture by camera is over.

Now, the Wayback Machine flings me forward to 1988 where I'm circling my daughter and her prom date in our living room with a 35mm camera in my hands. I can't help myself. Father genes are running the show.

A few minutes earlier, John, Emily's date, had appeared at our front door, knocked, and everyone in the living room had rearranged themselves like molecules of heated gas. We jumped back, sat down, stood up, and then jerked ourselves into attitudes of utter casualness.

There was another teenager, a younger brother. If there isn't a younger brother or sister, one must be rented for the evening. The junior sibling's job is to point out that everyone in the family has lost his or her mind.

At the first quiet, awkward moment, Junior must also say something inappropriate but true. He might look at the date's feet and say, "Your shoes *sure are big*."

My wife pinned the boutonniere to the lapel of John's tuxedo as I snapped the twenty-fourth and last frame of film.

I couldn't stop smiling. I was still grinning as the front door closed behind the prom-bound couple.

John was collecting my daughter in a 1972 Buick Electra 225 whose doors opened with torque pop. This ocean liner of a car would take John and Emily through their night of cheek-by-jowl conversation with long-stemmed, plastic champagne glasses from which they could not legally drink; key chains with large squares of plastic for prom pictures; miniature diploma holders with maroon, braided-twine straps for hanging from rearview mirrors; and dinner for two at the hands of a waiter who would spy them as soon as they entered the restaurant and mark them for persecution.

From the end of our driveway, came the sound of a goat with something lodged in its throat. The Buick didn't want to start.

Little brother and I slipped outside. Creeping like infantry scouts to the front of the house, we looked into the front yard, but the Detroit dreadnought no longer spanned the end of the driveway. John had started the car. He and Emily were underway in the interstellar traveler.

Junior and I dived for cover as the ship of the line, having floated down the street to turn around, began its run to the open sea. The Buick battlewagon required several seconds to pass. And, then, it was gone.

I walked to the end of the driveway in time to see the car's taillights, shining from sea to shining sea, round the corner, the same corner the Prom Princess turned on her way to the first grade.

Truck Repair,
a Revelation

When I bought my truck twenty-three years ago, I told the salesman it had to be standard transmission and that I didn't want air conditioning.

I must have been in one of those back-to-nature, better living through simplicity whim-whammies. Usually, that condition lasts one camping trip. This one would endure for almost a quarter of a century. I was still driving the truck the day Hurricane Katrina dropped a tree on it.

The truck had to be special ordered. I awaited delivery in a shimmering state of self-righteousness. That mechanical virtue lasted for years. I did my own tune-ups and oil changes. No longer was I at the mercy of garage mechanics who greeted customers with, "Say, neighbor, what can I do you for?" I particularly hated that bit of homespun since the mechanics meant exactly that.

When I crawled under the truck on a summer afternoon, hands clutching crescent wrench, filter wrench, and dirty oil catcher, the cool shade beneath the pickup felt like church, a place of worship where the occasional cat walked through. I scraped some knuckles but never once put new oil in the engine without remembering to put the drain plug back in.

In time, I came to trust a garage a few blocks from our house. It was easy to turn over maintenance to mechanics who appreciated the roominess and simplicity of working on my truck. With a six-cylinder engine and no air conditioner, there was room under the hood for a reading lamp and an easy chair.

Because I'd worked on the truck myself, I assumed a knowledge of its working parts that I didn't possess. I became one of those men who *knows* what's wrong with his car and hands the mechanic a list of possible solutions.

"I'm pretty sure it's the 1) Alternator, 2) Fuel pump or filter, 3) Water pump, 4) Radiator hose (never the radiator, too expensive), 5) Brake pads, 6) Linkage (standard transmission), 7) Fluid level (automatic transmission), or 8) Heater core."

The next time you tell the mechanic at the front desk what's wrong with your vehicle, ask him to let you see what he's written on the work order.

In mechanic's pencil scrawl will be the words, "Customer *thinks* it's the heater core."

A few months ago, I had a funny smell in the truck. I hadn't been fishing or raiding curbside trash piles, so I knew it wasn't me or anything left under the seat. The smell could only be a leaking heater core, I decided. The odor got so ripe that friends insisted we go to lunch in *their* cars.

Along with the keys to the truck, I handed Winston, the mechanic at the counter that morning, a note written in ballpoint and ripped from a pad, "Strong smell. Check for coolant leaking from radiator heater core."

"We'll give you a call after a while," the mechanic said.

I hadn't been back home an hour when the telephone rang.

"Ready to roll," Winston said.

"How much?" I asked.

"No charge."

"Was it the heater core?"

"It was a lizard."

The way Winston said, "It was a lizard," I knew the leaking reptile scraped from the doorframe had already been enshrined in the garage's Complaint Hall of Fame.

Leaf Blowing

My wife, who is smarter than I am, is forever tricking me into doing things I don't want to do.

"Would you please rake the leaves?" she asked the other day. "Use the leaf blower. Take a minute."

She knows I hate raking leaves. So she says, "I'll blow the leaves if you'll pick them up." She climbs onto the house to blow the leaves from the roof. She hops down to blow the leaves into enormous piles. Then, she goes inside to watch a show on cable television that gives women tips on getting men off the couch.

It takes me hours to pick up all the leaves my wife has effortlessly blown into piles. I could dispose of the leaves in minutes if there weren't all these rules governing where I may and may not put the leaves. I may not, for instance, pile the leaves in the long, fern bed beside the house. In the past, ferns and cats have reappeared by spring, so what's the big deal? Leaves may not be piled higher than any tree or azalea bush in the yard. Leaves may not be blown into the street to return on the next in-shore wind.

Leaves *must* be either bagged or laboriously transported to the compost pile. Let's make this difficult, shall we? Raking leaves slows time to the point that time begins to move backward. You might be forty when you start raking on a Saturday afternoon and just learning to walk by the time you finish.

That would be fine if raking leaves were fun, which it isn't. Homeowners are miserly when it comes to paying neighborhood kids to rake leaves but hand over fists full of $5 bills for mowing the lawn. A mowed yard looks like a complete job. A raked yard is just a yard awaiting more leaves.

So, we take it out on the poor children. The Kids Union of Lawnmower Operators, the most powerful labor group in the United States, sets the minimum for mowing a yard at $10. The yard may be no larger than a doormat. Ten bucks. The union rate for raking leaves, on the other hand, is $100 an hour. That is why adults rake their own leaves or make young, non-union children do the job.

When I was about ten, I agreed to rake a yard the size of a cow pasture for fifty cents. Until that day, my little sister thought me a bright big brother, someone she could turn to for advice.

"Fifty cents?!" she cried. "Are you crazy? It's going to take all year to rake this stupid yard."

She was right. We had been raking for an hour, with little to show for it, when the lady of the house descended the front steps with a suitcase in either hand.

"Hey, where ya going?" my sister bawled.

"To Chicago," the woman called back. "I'll pay you next month."

Seconds after the woman's car rounded the corner, we took off. I never walked by that house again. I ran. It was that or don a yellow wig and large fake eyeglasses.

I was having flashbacks to the fifty-cent leaf job the other day as I slung the leaf blower's strap over my shoulder, the way I'd seen my wife do. Unlike my wife, who is the Van Cliburn of leaf blowing, I have never gotten the hang of high-tech leaf rearrangement. My problem lies in not remembering that, once turned on, the machine is designed to imitate the exhaust of a jet engine. I no sooner got the leaves organized into piles than I turned and blasted the neat piles back into individual leaves.

I got so frustrated I called in all the preschoolers on the street. I gave them each a dime to take armloads of leaves to *their* yards.

"We'll be in the union this time next year," one of the tykes muttered.

I thought to give him a blast of air from the leaf blower, but I didn't. The look on his face said, "You'll need me one day when your back is out and you can't find your car for the leaves."

Welcome to
the Pack

It's late when I switch off the bedside lamp. Our daughter has been in labor for more than twenty hours. Sure that I'll be awakened by a jangling telephone before dawn, I roll onto my side and sleep. I awake to early morning light illuminating half the bedroom. A thunderstorm is gathering strength. I sit up with a start. It's 6:30 a.m. No call. She has been in labor close to twenty-eight hours. Enough.

Making coffee, I kill a little time before calling Austin for the fifth time in twenty-four hours. "Labor and delivery," a voice says.

"Labor Room 68," I say.

Silence on the line. I hold my breath. Please, God.

"Hold, please. They just had a baby in there."

Then, I'm standing alone in my kitchen crying. My wife comes on the line. She's crying. She hands the telephone to my daughter, who has just given birth to a boy weighing almost ten pounds. Emily is crying. Michael, her husband, is crying.

"Everyone in here is crying," my wife announces.

A few minutes later, having heard Cullen's glorious wail, I hang up the telephone. I wander into the living room to find water cascading from the top of a doorjamb. Backed up drain channel on the roof. Minutes later, I'm on the roof with a broom clearing the drain when lightning strikes close enough to make my skin tingle. The leaves on the live oak limbs hanging over the house become hundreds of little audio speakers.

A voice says: *I have made you a grandfather. Mother and child are fine. Do not push your luck.*

Back inside, I pull up rugs, mop, soak up water from the carpeting with towels. The doorjamb no longer drips water. This morning has been etched into memory like deep cursive writing in heavy crystal. I head for the office.

Three days later, I'm a passenger in my son's automobile heading west. We feel like pilgrims traveling to a faraway shrine. Yes, we are on our way to see the Miracle Child of the Condo. My son-in-law has told me that his child has enormous hands, Horowitzian mitts. "He has his mother's hands."

I regard my son's hands on the steering wheel. Huge hands. I glance at my hands and laugh. The new person's hands will one day dwarf mine, too.

The baby is equal parts Winston Churchill, Smurf, and Cochise. And beautiful. The genes have been nicely distributed. He looks like at least several people on each side of his family. I cannot decide which fills me more with wonder—holding the baby or watching my daughter hold the baby. I enjoy watching my son and my wife's brother hold the baby. This is funny. Holding a baby, young people look older, older people look younger.

When the other grandparents arrive, they take turns holding the baby. We all take turns nuzzling the baby. At this moment, there is not fifteen minutes' evolutionary difference between us and wolves.

Fishing with Malcolm

You almost never see a TV fisherperson with his jacket treble hooked to his pants.

Oh, you'll see a pro television fisherperson miss a bass when he or she tries to set the hook and yell something that has to be bleeped, but you never see the good stuff on the TV fishing shows.

Years after a fishing trip, it's not the fish you remember but the motor falling off or losing a favorite rod over the side or your buddy falling out of the boat as he reached for an ice cold Old Flugie.

One glorious spring day, Malcolm and I were fishing Big Ray's pond. We set up camp with an ice chest altar of fancy crackers, tins of sardines, Vienna sausage, and cashews.

You never see fishing snacks on the TV shows, but the reason men and women fish is to stop at some hole-in-the-wall bait stand for potato chips, beer, soft drinks, Slim Jims, and cheap cigars.

At your finer holes in the wall, the cheap cigars are sold from the same shelf as cheap gin, fresh packs of playing cards, and dice sealed in plastic cubes.

Convenience store clerks say the cheap cigars are expensive because kids hollow them out for the smoking of dope. If you believe this, then the clerks are saying that cheap cigars fetch a premium because a lot of dope is getting smoked in them. Have peace accords been signed in the war on drugs?

After a couple of casts to ripples near the bank, a fish-catching window of about thirty minutes opened, and I got very busy catching large bream and small bass on an ultra-light rod and reel.

That's when I became attached to my pants.

I'd tried to set the hook when a bass hit the Heddon Tiny Torpedo on my line. A Tiny Torpedo is a top-water lure that's been around since my father fished. James Heddon designed his first lures around 1900.

Zing came the Tiny Torpedo back at me after my yank failed to hook the bass. The lure embedded itself in the lining of my jacket. I wasn't about to stop fishing, so I clipped the line and left the lure dangling from the jacket.

When the fish stopped biting, I tried to rise from my bass-catching crouch to find the lure hooked to my jacket *and* my heavy, canvas pants.

"What's the matter? Your back go out?" Malcolm asked, as I approached camp bent over.

"I'm hooked to my pants," I said.

After Malcolm freed me of the treble hooks with wire snips from his tackle box, we sat in camp to watch the trees absorb the last light of day. Afternoon became evening. We sat beside the pond until it was so dark we could only *hear* the bass jumping.

On the way home, we decided to dine at the Fleur de Lis, a neighborhood restaurant renowned for its square pizzas. A tipsy woman who thought she knew Malcolm told us all about herself. Finally, she realized she didn't know Malcolm. She'd mistaken him for Stephen King, the horror book writer.

Malcolm took the fish because he felt like cleaning them, and I didn't. The TV fishing shows would have you believe that a day on the water should end in a $150-a-night fishing lodge before a log fire. Stopped at the first red light, full to the eyebrows with pizza, I felt just fine.

The Heart Volcano

A fruit fly entry has won the local science fair. I feel the losers' relief.

The mere mention of Science Fair and I'm thirteen, standing in the corner of a gymnasium sweating into my Easter suit. Down the line of projects the judges advance, past miniature plants for the desalination of seawater, working models of nuclear power plants, and an exhibit outlined in white lights titled "How I Solved World Hunger" by Biff Brilliant, age twelve.

On the judges come, down the narrow streets of Science Fair Shanty Town, past plywood constructions of gaudy paint, letters and numbers carved from balsa wood, and shining, silver cylinders linked one to the other with brass tubes. My armpits are The Tivoli Fountain as I anticipate the judges' reactions to my late Sunday afternoon contribution to science.

The project was the evolutionary zenith of all my other lame efforts. With the announcement that our science fair entries were due in three months, the conscientious among us began genetically altering hamsters and fruit flies. The rest of us daydreamed the best projects ever. Then, we forgot about the science fair until the Sunday afternoon before the Monday that our projects were due.

"Don't you have a science fair project due soon?" my mother asked.

My blood slowed to an icy trickle.

My last minute, pathetic efforts in grammar school and junior high were usually human hearts done in modeling clay with black sewing thread stretched semi-tautly to mark the left and right ventricles and the aorta. Veins were thin, blue, spaghetti-like strands of clay stuck to the hapless heart. It is heartbreaking to stay up all night crafting in clay an actual, non-working human heart only to be blown away by flies that have had sex.

After my science teacher promised a grade of "F" to the next human heart, I switched to The Erupting Volcano, though I knew I'd still end up on the short row of shame reserved for last minute works in clay. We'd stand once more under the sullied banner in Craven Corner.

Then, genius borne of nothing-else-to-lose guided my hands to merge the cliches of science projects into a work of art, a poem to procrastination and a protest against mandatory, meaningless science fair projects.

Next to the orbital rockets, human brains encased in plastic, and some fourteen-year-old's solution to a thousand-year-old math problem, my greatest work stood as a squat monument to life in the real world.

Dumping half a box of baking soda into a jagged hole in the clay and pouring vinegar, I cried, "Distinguished Judges, Gentlemen and Lady, I give you . . . The Heart Volcano!"

The volcano's aorta erupted with a mighty spewing noise. The lady judge gasped and the men shielded their eyes. There was a wet, gloppy "Boom!" Then . . . silence in the cavernous gymnasium.

The applause started low and built as the judges stomped off in their splattered suits and dress. My fellow students began to twirl in mad delight.

The Scientists of Craven Corner knew victory for the first time. It tasted of baking soda and dusty clay. Sweet.

Letter in a Woodpile

The skin on one forearm is dappled with an intriguing rash I must have gotten carrying firewood. It is a small price to pay for working in spring sunshine.

Working alone (a friend in hailing distance on the porch), I have sawed, carried, and stacked wood for an hour or so. Maybe longer. My wristwatch is on the big table in the dining room.

I have placed wood and kindling on the pile near the back door of the farmhouse and in so doing have left a love note for my son. When he reads this, he may telephone to say in his terse way, "You could have just said 'note.'" But it was a love note that I left him.

My wife's family sold some land to the government in the late 1940s. They used the money to build the house at The Farm. Those builders are dead, but they live on in bits of Indian pottery and arrowheads they collected on the land and in an insurance calendar from a company that went the way of the Indians. The clothes, books, games, tools, report cards, and ledgers of the departed linger in closets whose doors are hard to open when the weather is wet.

The wooden floors have known the bare feet of cousins, their children, grandchildren, great-grandchildren. When I am alone in the house, I can hear my grandson's small bare feet stomping the living room floor. He'd been walking but a short time his first visit to the house.

I see the boy's father look up from the novel he was reading, call his son "Stompy," and look back down at the paragraph he'd read three times.

The fireplace in the big room is the house's only heat, except for a cranky stove in the kitchen that is older than the cousins who now pay the property tax.

It is doubtful than anyone has ever been in danger of freezing in this house, fire or no fire. The technology of modern sleeping bags would see one safely through the coldest nights. But a fire on a cold, deep winter night or an evening in early spring (especially in a drizzling rain) is so civilized.

To have a fire when the mood or the weather demands one, you must plan ahead. That isn't always easy when the afternoon is warm and the drone of bees and bump, bump of flies against a wood frame door say, "Nap. Close your eyes. Sleep."

Standing in blue jeans (one more day and they'll walk themselves back to the house) and T-shirt, I pull the bow saw through limbs that fell in a late December ice storm.

If I cut a little wood each afternoon, I provide fires for evenings unimagined. When I tire, I go inside to fix a cup of coffee or fish a cold beer from the refrigerator. It's an extravagance, but if open windows have chilled the air a bit inside the house, I build a small fire and sit to stare as the kindling catches.

Sometimes, my son uses wood from the pile to build fires for himself and friends. When I work the wood, cutting and dragging, chopping, sawing and stacking, I talk to him, though he's wearing a tie in a city hundreds of miles away.

"I won't be around when you burn this wood. May I suggest using the stuff, here, because it's oldest and needs to be burned before it rots.

"Should you arrive in the middle of the night and want a fire, I'd recommend this wood, here, because it's driest and most slender and will catch quickly.

"I know you'll build your fires to suit yourself. But look here. I've put some kindling inside a plastic bag and stuck it inside this vault of logs.

"This wood is green. Mix it with seasoned wood for coals that last."

I enjoy the company and conversation of my son, but the woodpile is hard to beat for purity of communication. Our arrangement of sticks and sawed limbs is unambiguous talk: "Hello. How are you? I hope you enjoy your time here as much as your mother and I did."

Block That Stress!

Our first night at stress management class, Karen, the instructor, asked us to name some signs of stress.

"Headache," offered a young mother.

"Stomachache," said an older woman.

"DIA-REE-YA!" boomed a man through cupped hands on the front row.

The room, deep in the, uh, bowels of a hospital, got quiet. The man broke the silence by laughing too hard.

Karen, who could be the model for one of Maxfield Parrish's damoiselles, smiled, "Yes, that's right. Diarrhea *is* a symptom of stress. Very good."

Karen is a yoga disciple. You could wrap a watchband around her middle and buckle it on the third hole. Outwardly, Karen is everything her students are not. She is one with the universe. Her stressed-wracked students arrive from outer space in wicker baskets.

It looked like the last time a cookie had crossed Karen's lips was when she was five. She told us how important diet is in stress management. As she talked about the horror of coffee, the depravity of sugar, the calamity that is cola, we stared past her to the snack table the hospital had thoughtfully provided. Awaiting our break were cans of cola under ice in a huge glass bowl, four kinds of cookies, and a metal container of coffee the size of a water tower. Karen was outdone. She placed her hands on perfect hips and tapped an immaculate foot. She was tempted "to just call housekeeping" and have them take "this awful junk food away." Karen changed her mind when we threw back our heads and began barking like arctic foxes.

Gentle Karen's methods of dealing with stress were invented on Tarragonia, the invisible fourth planet from the sun. Stress was eliminated on Tarragonia before earth's pyramids were built. The running stress dogs in Karen's class understood the theory of stress reduction. What we didn't understand was how it applied to us.

Karen asked us to rate our stress on a scale of one to ten. The class average was fourteen. Karen told a man in his mid-50s that he shouldn't worry about how others saw him. The way he saw *himself* was the important thing.

"Karen, you don't understand," the man said. "These people are out to get me. These people want to fire me, Karen."

One night, a couple of weeks into the class, Karen asked us if we had done our stress management homework. We hung our heads. We tugged at our forelocks. We feared Karen might have the cookies and cola removed. On those nights of heavy gravity, Karen didn't scold. She took us through a relaxation exercise. Karen hadn't gotten through the second step before the entire class was sleeping soundly.

Early in the five-week course, I began watching a young mother and the older woman who sat next to her beneath the room's thermostat. My stress was baby stuff compared to the young mother's. I enjoyed the classes. The young woman looked upon them as escape from crazed butterflies. She and the older woman became good friends. One night, it was cold enough in the room to safely keep pork. The friends fooled with the thermostat until the room was so warm people were falling out of their chairs. We were dreaming before we hit the floor.

"Whew," Karen said. "Is it just me? Or is it *hot* in here?"

The friends giggled like schoolgirls. The rest of us were grumpy as hell when we came to on the floor. We downed some more coffee and cookies.

Karen told us there are little stress generators inside each of us. The stress is always there. It's not stress that wacks us out but "stress triggers." Karen told us there are certain people in the world who are "stress carriers." I made a quick list of the "stress carriers" in my life. I had to ask Karen for more paper, which she cheerfully provided.

I missed the last class. The day was so hectic I had to stay late to finish some work. It would have been too stressful to try to make stress class. Karen understood when I called to apologize.

Years later, I wonder what became of Karen. Does she sail on, immaculate in her quietude? Does she have bad days in traffic that put her in Warrior Pose against the horn of her car? I opt for serene Karen, mistress of stress class, a woman who could ignore a cookie but permit the less evolved theirs.

Tiger Charge

It doesn't matter if it's Tiger Woods or some amateur. I know that smile on golfers' faces as they accept the gallery's applause.

The golfers seem surprised that a few thousand people have been following them around. They touch the bills of their caps, smile sheepishly, and walk on. I know that smile because it is the smile that I used to see on the face of my friend, Jimmy, as we competed in golf and track and field in our back yards.

Were our smiles copies of ones we'd seen on "Wide World of Sports" or outward manifestations of deep happiness? I think the latter.

We played backyard golf with baseball bats and baseballs. We used the fat part of the bat to drive. We used the lip of wood at the other end of the bat to chip, lifting the ball from high grass. Putting with the fat end of the bat was decidedly safer, but using the lip of the bat was more satisfying, unless the ball sailed into the circular hedge or bounced off the woodpile.

Jimmy's skill as a pole-vaulter in our backyard Olympics stands out in my memory despite the remarkable heights today's vaulters achieve. Sure, they go higher than Jimmy did, but they're using high-tech poles. Jimmy used a rusting television antenna mast. Our version of the event added weight-lifting to the vault.

That backyard competitive feeling comes back when I watch high stakes golf matches on television. I like to watch golf while Nordic Tracking. The pastoral game is excellent with the sound turned off and Jimi Hendrix blasting on the stereo. On the other hand, televised baseball is best viewed while ironing shirts and listening to Mozart.

Cablevision once had a show early in the morning for people who exercise on machines. My favorite segment featured bicycle riders climbing a mountain pass. No sound. Just a stopwatch showing you the passage of seconds and minutes. Wonderful television. Golf on television is good viewing, too, as prelude to afternoon napping. That's how I, a nongolfer, got hooked on televised golf matches in the first place.

I was snuggling down for a Sunday afternoon nap during the Masters Golf Tournament that launched Tiger Woods. I couldn't nod off for watching Woods' charge. Golfers don't really "charge." Breathy announcers say that because it sounds better than, "It just doesn't get any better than this. Tiger Woods is 'walking' into the lead."

In one British Open, a golf course in Scotland was described as a "brute" and a "beast." Players feared a "bashing" and a "beating" from sand, water, wind, and grass. Golf may drive a player around the bend, but golfers rarely suffer concussions or broken collarbones unless they fall into a sand trap or walk, make that "charge," into a tree.

When Tiger Woods proved to be human and "collapsed" in a tournament, no medics rushed onto the links. Had he been playing football, he'd have been rushed to the hospital. This was golf. Tiger retired to the clubhouse, feeling badly, no doubt, but not requiring surgery.

For Cat's Sake

She was an outside cat who, after more than fourteen years of dodging moving vans, delivery trucks, and cars, seemed to grow old in a single day.

Dubbed "Scat Cat" by the children, she was Mama Cat to my wife and me. We'd let Mama Cat have a litter of kittens before we had her fixed. She'd had the litter in an outdoor closet that had a square cut out of the door near the bottom.

Our children built walls of cardboard and castoff plywood to corral the kittens in a breezeway outside the closet. There, children and kittens passed summer days in a tangle of T-shirts, shorts, bare limbs, and fur on cool cement. When Mama Cat had had it with our children, she'd pick up hers to carry them through the hole in the door.

The breezeway and outdoor closet disappeared in a renovation years ago, but I saw the arrangement clearly in mind's eye the other afternoon as I dug a grave for Mama Cat at a corner of the house.

My wife and I were trying to be matter of fact about the cat's death. She had lived a long time, given us pleasure, lowering our blood pressures as we watched her asleep in the shade, draped—a Dali cat—across the seat of a wrought-iron chair.

There are other cats buried in the yard. Each of us has a mental map of where the cats are buried. Whoever buries a cat puts up a crude wooden cross. Sawed-up tomato stakes make sturdy, light crosses. The pointed end is a bonus. The cross makes the burial party feel better, but the crosses don't stand long. The surface space is needed. A cherished cat's resting place becomes foundation for a pile of kindling or a pot of marjoram, and the seasons roll one into the next.

When my son stopped by the other night, I told him Mama Cat had died and that I'd buried her, careful not to disturb the resting places of other cats.

"You know," he said, "one of the shed's posts is about a foot out of line with the other posts because of Oddibe."

My son built the shed, digging the post holes and placing the posts by himself. One of the holes, he realized, would disturb the grave of Oddibe. I named a long-ago cat Oddibe after the Texas Ranger outfielder Oddibe McDowell. Careers of the cat and the outfielder were brief. The posthole pattern was slightly off, I realized, to accommodate a cat's eternal lounging place.

Mama Cat lay against the side of the house behind some ferns all one afternoon. We kept checking to make sure she was dead. I dug a grave and buried her under a hydrangea's long, curving branches and big blue Kleenex blossoms.

My wife and children know the family cats' genealogy the way an old aunt can recite the names of relatives. When I hear the histories of the cats, I am reminded of the almost separate life I lead.

I can name city officials back to the 1970s. I remember many of the police jurors, constables, sheriffs, and aldermen I last saw in action twenty years ago. I remember the way the road looked on a golden afternoon in the Sabine Wildlife Refuge twenty-five years ago, and I remember where I stopped for lunch that day.

But I cannot name all the cats. I don't remember certain people who lived on our street, people my wife says I spoke to more than once, let alone the names of pets.

"You remember those people," my wife will say. "They lived in Shane and Amy's house before the Nidas."

I was at work the day the LSU bull found our dead-end street. I didn't see the little army of lariat-twirling cops nor the bull's confrontation with Meredith's mother's dachshund. I didn't see the bull enter the Waller's garage to hide from the yapping dog, gear-flapping police, and the arm-waving mothers of gleeful children.

All these memories and partial memories and other people's memories wrapped me up as I leaned on the posthole digger to wipe sweat from my eyes.

I buried Mama Cat, pushed dirt onto the grave with the toe of a shoe, packed the earth with the back of the shovel blade, and went in to supper.

Aroma Inventory

I step from the chilled, sterile air of a drugstore into the moist, muscular heat of Louisiana summer.

I can feel the asphalt's blaze through the soles of my shoes. It's tempting to drive home in air-conditioned comfort. Instead, I drive the six blocks with windows down to take an inventory of aromas.

The chemical plants above and below Baton Rouge on the Mississippi River pump smells into the air that range from just-plain stink to smells that suggest all the flavors in a plastic sack of Jolly Ranchers.

Some mornings, the air is heavy with the smell of roasting coffee from the Community Coffee plant across the river. The smell is strong enough to *be* that second cup of coffee.

As the air heats up and the humidity mounts to ninety percent, it's not flowers you smell so much as it is everything else.

One afternoon, dripping from mowing the yard, I sat in the shade drinking ice water, and the smell of Tanker, the yardman of my childhood, ambled up.

Tanker worked hard in the summer and didn't bathe unnecessarily. His smell was more than human. He smelled liked a rotting tree in the woods, the edge of a bayou, a pile of leaves. He smelled liked the oil on the

his push lawnmower. He smelled of sweat-
hakis, ruined felt hat, and big leather shoes
had pushed over to look like speedboats making
tight turns.

I imagined that Tanker smelled like the pioneers in
my school books.

I think of Tanker and I think of the summer smells
of long ago — heat rising through crape myrtle blossoms
at street's edge, storm drains, the exhaust of passing cars,
wet dogs. When the air was still and hot, you could smell
a woman's perfume above the sidewalk three minutes
after she'd walked by.

At noon and again toward evening, a menu of
aromas opened. The Schmidts were having pork chops.
Miss Irene was frying okra. Someone's roux for gumbo
was about to burn.

To grow up in South Louisiana is to know a
laboratory of competing smells. New Orleans is the
smell of restaurants and jasmine on courtyard walls;
also, the sweet, sickening smell of garbage, sewage,
and diapered horses pulling sweating tourists in
white carriages.

You learn to smell rain before it arrives. You learn
to tell the different smells of rain on concrete, brick, and
iron. There's no comparing the smell of rain through a
wrought iron grill and the way rain smells when you
inhale wet air through a screened door.

I'm almost home from the drugstore when the
odor of ligustrum slaps my nose. I park the car in
the driveway and walk toward the house through
the perfume of dangling ginger blossoms. At the front
door, I stop to sniff. The smell of pork roast says, "Come
on in."

Home Schooling

If I learned anything at L. S. Rugg Grammar School, and certainly I did, it must have been before lunch.

After lunch, my body was at my desk, but my mind soared free outside the tall, narrow windows set in the walls that held us prisoners to instruction.

At my desk, the kind that was screwed to the floor, seat snugged up to a hinged writing surface, I dreamed large. There was a deep gouge at the top of the desk that held a No. 2 pencil sharpened to lethal pointedness. And there was an ink well in the upper right corner of the desk that once held a bottle of ink that belonged to me.

I never dipped a girl's pigtails in the ink well as my Uncle Bill said he'd done. One, a girl with pigtails never sat in front of me. Two, a classmate had had a spectacular accident involving a new Esterbrook pen and the aforementioned bottle of ink. Three, there was my mother's admonition to *never*, but *never*, act on any suggestion from my Uncle Bill.

"Your Uncle Bill is *not* an example you should follow," my mother often said.

I loved my Uncle Bill. He taught me to drive. He took me to the country where I could shoot my BB gun. He coerced bartenders into paying me top price for the Coke bottles I saved by the hundreds in our garage.

Bolted to the floor it may have been, but that school desk carried me far away on warm, sleepy afternoons. I knew other children had sat at that desk imagining that they sailed with Columbus, dined with the Pilgrims, and stood in the crowd at Gettysburg. The sun dropped toward dismissal time, and I drew spaceships, war engines, advanced fighter planes, and lethal submarines. I drew U.S. Army tanks and German Panzers that fired dashed lines at one another.

Lifting the sharpened pencil from its convenient groove, I would turn to a fresh page in a loose-leaf notebook. And I'd draw. To this day, a pristine, lined page holds out promise to me. It can be a list of things I mean to do, a diagram for a fall garden, a drawing of a shed that I might build if one could build a shed with a pencil.

The teacher droned on about Tonti of the Iron Hand or introduced an idea in arithmetic or lectured on the shipping tonnage on the Great Lakes, and I drew. I knew the supersonic spy plane would end up as an extension ladder laid across wooden Coke crates. And that the cockpit would be my baby sister's old highchair seat after I'd ripped it out of the previous week's submarine chaser.

I was wrapped in the power of possibility even as I stepped into the reality of our double-bay garage and saw not the Wright Brothers' bicycle shop but ranks of dusty, dark green glass bottles held in reserve by me for the Coca-Cola Bottling Co.

Was my enthusiasm diminished? Slightly. I did the best I could with what lay in the garage as imagination reasserted itself. Then, my mother called me to dinner from the window of the back bedroom. I went inside to eat, did homework, and went to bed. In the seconds before sleep, a bi-plane, PT boat, or dirigible took shape in the garage. I could hear the faint cheers of enthusiastic Coke bottles as an expanse of canvas fell away from my latest creation.

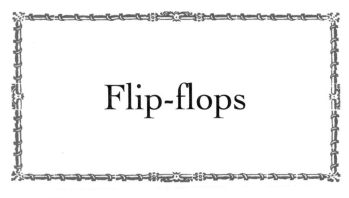

Flip-flops

Buying new flip-flops signals the start of summer for me.

Those slabs of rubber in lime green, strawberry red, plum purple, and the ever-popular basic black are cooler than a watermelon buried in a tub of ice.

Flip-flops were once considered beach wear and summer house shoes. I got my first pair in junior high school gym class. We wore flip-flops in the shower to ward off mutant athlete's foot.

Today, people wear flip-flops wherever they want. A friend who coordinates weddings at the cathedral downtown says, "They get married in them. They have little heels and sequins, but they're still flip-flops."

Almost gone is the sound of screened, wooden doors creaking open to be yanked closed by long, coiled springs. Where's the once familiar "slick-slick" sound of the motorless lawnmower?

Flip-flops survive as sounds of summer whether they're slapping the heels of swimsuit models or the feet of small children following dogs down tree-shaded sidewalks. The sound of flip-flops gives us the weight and importance of an announced arrival.

In the winter, I walk an old part of Baton Rouge called Beauregard Town. I walk fast for exercise in high-tech running shoes. In the summer, those streets are walked best in flip-flops, slowly, the better to look at houses from another century wrapped in electric blue morning glory blossoms.

A professor of music at LSU named Bill Grimes gets some friends together each summer to play jazz concerts. The audiences are young and old jazz enthusiasts. The older concert goers arrive in summer dresses, a few in heels. Their escorts wear ties, jackets, and dress shoes.

The young people show up in whatever they put on that morning. A few minutes before the music starts, they sashay in wearing T-shirts, cutoff jeans — and flip-flops.

Those so shod aren't shunned.

Everyone slides down in his or her chair as the music floats out from the stage.

Moms and pops.

Those in flip-flops.

Dig the bebop.

The Elgin

I'm working in the yard on a hot summer afternoon, blink the sweat out of my eyes, and there's my long-dead father with a Flit gun. My father would ram the gun's plunger into a long, skinny metal tube to produce a fine, blue-gray mist of death. Then, the mist would slowly drift back onto my father. He'd wave away the little cloud of insecticide with one hand, shake the Flit with the other hand, and fire again. Looking at the bites on my baby sister's arms, it was easy to see that my father received more bug spray than the bugs.

I blink again and my father is bent over an Elgin outboard motor he'd clamped to the rim of a metal garbage can filled with water. There must have been a time when my father clamped the Elgin to the back of a boat. My memories of the $1^1/2$ horsepower engine and its flaking green paint are confined to the garbage can lagoon.

We rarely fished together, but we spent hours with the Elgin under a sycamore tree in the backyard. My father would carefully wind a length of dirty cotton rope around a small, notched wheel in the top of the outboard, then heave mightily. Many heaves were necessary to wring the motor to life.

The "brup-brup" sound of the gasoline engine's firing was a happy sound—if you weren't on the business end of the rope.

I can see the look of joy on my father's face when the motor finally coughed, caught, and began churning the water in the garbage can. We'd stand looking at the excited Elgin like primitive men tending a shrine. We had posed a question. The gods were answering.

Bits of cabbage, coffee grounds, eggshells, and bread swirled in the prop wash. My father could be relied upon to say something like, "Gives the garbage can a good cleaning." Like there was a reason for what we were doing.

The outboard would run for about a minute, then quit. Or the cotter pin would break, and we'd have to lift the Elgin out of the garbage can to fit a new piece of twisted lead to the propeller shaft.

The sound that now disturbs the heavy afternoon air is my neighbor's string trimmer. I sink dripping into a chair in the shade. In the heated air that shimmers above the street, I see a man standing beside a racing outboard engine. He's younger than I am and smiling. I know him.

The Hurricane Game

South Louisiana loves a hurricane that misses. The relationship between hurricane and homeowner is like the dance between bull and matador. It's a thrill to flirt with danger until horn or storm strikes home.

We don't wish hurricanes on anyone, but the beatings we've taken from the big storms let us appreciate the suspense of trying to guess where a hurricane will hit. Great storms like Andrew, Katrina, and Rita remind us that while the odds of a hurricane hitting a particular place are long, the suffering and damage are immense when the big ones hit.

Late on the evening of Aug. 25, 1992, I walked away from a birthday party in my honor to look at the leafy limbs of a big gum tree waving over the house. Hurricane Andrew had torn up South Florida two days earlier and was now drawing a bead on the Louisiana coast.

By the next morning, it seemed certain that Baton Rouge, too, would remember Andrew.

Though more than a hundred miles from the Gulf at the closest point, we had trees down all over town. Our neighborhood was without electricity for a week. We spent the hours of daylight getting ready for the night, pulling defrosting food from our freezers—steaks, seafood, frozen vegetables, breads, and soups.

We cooked on charcoal grills in our front yards. Dinner on our street moved from house to house each night. We followed our noses to the next feast. Each morning, my wife and I made coffee on a propane stove on the deck and ate defrosting English muffins heated on a camping toaster. Shane and Amy, neighbors who were sleeping in a tent in their backyard, would smell the coffee and walk over, Amy wrapped in a sheet.

For years, any talk of Andrew was sure to include a mention of English muffins and those morning get-togethers on our deck.

Hurricane season starts June 1 and runs through November. It is a time of wary watching and reliving other storms we've known or heard about. A hurricane killed between 6,000 and 8,000 people in Galveston September 8, 1900. A storm known as the "Hurricane of Independence" killed an estimated 4,000 people from North Carolina to Nova Scotia in September 1776.

An unnamed storm—hurricanes weren't named until 1953—is known in my family as the hurricane that almost killed Mildred, my mother. She was an infant asleep on a bed in front of a brick fireplace. As the house began to shake hard, someone picked her up and headed for the back door. Walls and roof began to part. The chimney fell across the bed where, seconds before, my mother had slept.

In the kitchen, Aggie was begging her brother, Floyd, to put down a large statue of the Virgin Mary and pick her up. Floyd had scooped up the statue from its place in the living room during his nervous pacing.

"Hold me, Floyd!" Aggie cried as the roof began to lift. My Uncle Floyd picked up his sister with one arm and, with the Virgin Mary under his other arm, ran for the back door. He cleared the steps, ran across the yard, and hurdled a fence. The height of the fence has risen over the years. It now qualifies my late uncle for the Olympics.

People on the Gulf and Atlantic coasts know August and September as dangerous months. Camille in 1969 and Betsy in 1965 came in August and September, respectively. Each did an estimated $1 billion in damage. After Katrina and Rita, recovery was no longer expressed in dollars but years.

When the hurricane season is young, don't get cocky. As the season matures, don't begin to breathe more easily. There's a tropical storm out there, somewhere, listening.

The Necessity
of Repetition

Wind chimes in the courtyard sound with an urgency in winter that isn't there in April.

"Urgency" is all in the head, of course. The wind chimes' musical clamor is urgent because I know a freeze is coming. First freeze in South Louisiana can come any time from late November to January. When it comes, it's the sound of the wind chimes in cold air that says "Freeze" as clearly as a voice on the radio.

The necessity of simple things repeating keeps us going. It doesn't hurt if these things are good, but they don't have to be. They can be nothings that make us smile or shake our heads. Implied is that if something repeats, there is life. Cancer cells repeat, but doctors and patients consult on schemes to beat the cancer. The treatments repeat for the good, we hope.

Mercy. This train of thought started as I washed plant trays before moving pots inside. Flipping a tray over this morning, I saw the words that make me laugh every winter.

"CLAY-COTTA." It's the brand name of a plastic plant tray that's cheaper than terracotta and lasts season after season. The good stuff gets broken and ends up as pieces in the bottoms of pots to assist drainage. There is a company name in raised plastic on the tray and a New York Fifth Avenue address. On the mornings before first freezes, I imagine well-heeled men and women madly turning out plastic plant trays on Fifth Avenue before rushing to lunch in places where plants sit in real cotta.

My front yard garden has been flooded with strong sunlight since I cut the Confederate rose to its base. Cousin of the hibiscus, the plant reached tree size before it became a white fly condo. The Confederate rose will be back in the spring, vigorous, white flies evicted.

Rows of evergreen onion, arugula, black-seeded Simpson lettuce, cilantro, and mustard greens applaud the giant hibiscus' demise. A windmill spins in the air, an eccentric shaft driving an iron cat to paw delicate shapes that may be sunflowers. The windmill's clatter over the garden and the pealing of wind chime tubes in the court-yard signal the coming of freezing cold.

Below the noisy metal cat, a volunteer morning glory vine climbs up hollyhocks to reach a wire fence. The morning glory climbs for sunlight, unmindful of freeze—reckless—bent on repetition.

Learning from a New Teacher

At some point, age becomes irrelevant between children and their parents. The child becomes adviser to the father. So, it is not surprising that my grandson, Cullen, has become my teacher. It's just that I didn't think it would happen before he got to the first grade.

When my daughter, who became my adviser sometime during middle school, told me to avoid a certain fast-food restaurant with Cullen, I should have listened.

Well, I did listen, but I chose to ignore what I heard. One rainy morning, I found myself Cullen's playmate for the day. And, then, it got to be lunchtime.

I remembered which burger restaurant to avoid, but I'd forgotten why. My undoing was the chain joint's playground equipment.

Cullen and I were in a town that wasn't Baton Rouge and wasn't Austin, which is where he lives. In other words, we were on neutral ground, except that there is no neutral ground when it comes to chain fast-food restaurants. They're all the same.

My grandson wanted to play in Burger World's covered playground. It occurred to me that the taking of sustenance ranked pretty low in Cullen's dining experience. The big things were the colors, height of the slides, and complexity of Burger World's playground.

I don't like those corporate playgrounds one bit. I'm afraid Cullen will crawl into one of the colored tubes, I'll see his face at the first plastic bubble portal, and that will be the last I see of my precious boy.

Poof. Gone. Disappeared. No more grandson. What will I tell his parents?

"I lost him. Well, I didn't lose him. The eighteen-year-old assistant manager at Burger World says Cullen is in there somewhere and that they'll find him sooner or later. In the meantime, they're shoving burgers, shakes, and fries up the slide with a pole." It's a conversation no father wants to have with his child about *her* child.

So, Cullen and I were sitting at one of those cute, blue tables that is just big enough for two burgers, two bags of fries, and two drinks when I noticed that my mentor had begun pinching the sesame seeds from the top of his bun.

Busted! Wrong burger joint. We were at Burger World. We were supposed to be at Burger Biggie where the buns are seedless.

As it turned out, the playground wasn't open because it was raining. Feeling guilty as I watched Cullen pinch away seeds and bread from his bun, I resolved to make amends. After he'd finished eating his meal in bits, we left in search of the other burger place.

Oh, we did get a toy at Burger World that both of us liked and enjoyed putting together. As I say, food ranks a distant second in the reasons children want to go to these burger places.

By the time we arrived at Burger Biggie, I had formulated a plan in which I, grandfatherly and pathetic, just like in the commercials, throw myself on the mercy of the teenager behind the counter.

I meant to drink coffee at one of the outside tables while Cullen played in the tubes. But the 19½-year-old manager nixed that plan with a shrug and his best corporate smile.

"Sorry, sir, the playground is closed because of the rain," the future CEO of Burger Biggie said.

I could have pointed out that the playground was covered and that the tubes were enclosed, but I didn't. I didn't want to hear about insurance liability or hear about Burger Biggie's corporate policy concerning rain and playgrounds.

"Cullen, we can't . . ." I began.

"It's OK, Pop. I don't *have* to play," said Cullen, hugging my leg.

I melted into a giant glob of yellow, processed cheese, amazed at the wisdom and compassion of someone so young and so short.

Back at the hotel where my grandson and I were taking a break from a family reunion, I let Cullen have the television's channel selector. He became enamored of the ever-repeating menu of the hotel's services. I turned back into his grandfather, hiding the selector when he wasn't looking. That threw him for about three seconds, the time it took him to figure out the buttons beneath the screen.

Life is a lot less frustrating when one knows when one is beaten. I stretched out on the bed and soon fell asleep to the recitation of offerings from room service.

The Attic Fan

"What *is* that?" a neighbor in her twenties asked, nodding at an attic fan lying atop a curbside trash pile.

"Before air conditioning," I said, "houses in the Deep South had attic fans. The fans drew air from outside through open windows. You threw a wall switch—*clack*!—and louvers in the hall ceiling cracked open as the fan rumbled to life."

"And it made you cool?" my neighbor asked.

"It was more the illusion of coolness," I said. "There was a breeze of wet air that carried the smell of dinner cooking next door and the fragrance of mown grass. And sound. Car tires on rain-wet pavement, roller skates on cement sidewalks, and the slick-slick-whirr of push lawnmowers.

Drinkable air swirled around you as it pulled damp coolness across your body. When you rose shirt-less from a Naugahyde couch, the sound and feeling of your skin leaving the furniture foretold the invention of Velcro.

Dampness and mold found leather shoes, belts, hats, wallpaper. Some houses radiated a smell of mold through their screen doors and windows. The smell was in the walls, rugs, members of the family and their pets.

My Uncle Floyd, who'd traveled out West, made a primitive air conditioner. He knocked together a wooden frame with screen on both sides. He filled the construction with hay and stuck the thing in the window in the spare bedroom. He tied the garden hose to the top of the frame and caused a slow drip to fall into the hay. He put a big, box fan on a chair to draw air through the wet hay.

"Did it work?" my neighbor asked.

"It was like napping beside Niagara Falls," I said.

Aunt Lucille made Uncle Floyd disconnect the water hose for fear a guest would be shocked to death in the electrified mist.

My room at home had big windows that slid on wooden tracks. On hot nights, I'd slide the windows back to reveal expanses of screen. With the powerful rush of air pressing against my face and flowing through my hair, I felt like Hornblower setting sail in the Hotspur.

Then, from the dark recesses of the house came the cries of my mother, father, sister as their bedrooms lost oxygen.

"Close those windows. NOW!" My poor mother, exhausted from a day of seeking and destroying mold.

My young neighbor had gotten a long answer to her question. I pushed the discarded fan with the tip of one shoe as we turned away from the trash pile. My wife would thank me for not bringing home something else to store in the shed.

I write this in T-shirt and shorts, chilled air moving over me from the central air-conditioning vents in the wall. I love the old days recalled in comfort.

Around Midnight

The moon is obscured by clouds. There is the smell of rain in the air, which probably means rain before morning. A weekday night, it's late. I'll head for bed when the mantel clock in the living room bongs faintly twelve times.

For the moment, however, one of the cats — we have several head on the place — shares space with me on the hood of the car. There is a glass of chilled wine within easy reach. The wine is mine. The cat, as far as I know, is a teetotaler.

The minutes before midnight often find me in the yard surveying my holdings. It's peaceful out here. Thunder and rain are hours away. The cat rubs his head on the bottoms of my bare feet. When he springs to the hood of the car, I move the wine to the other hand to rub the back of the cat's head, now butting my leg.

The light from a street lamp illuminates our front yard vegetable and herb garden. Hidden from the street by a short fence of wide planks and a banana tree, the garden surprises visitors who walk up from the street. Every cat in the neighborhood knows it's there.

The leaves of squash plants move in the rain-scented air, dipping and waving before tomato vines wrapped around stakes starting to lean with the weight. Tall, slender shallots topped by large, white seed balls stand watch along one side of the garden, sheltering lettuce and parsley seedlings.

Cucumbers stand aloof on their private hill, ready for an assault on the poplar trees bordering the far side of the garden. One year, I had to borrow a neighbor's ladder to harvest the tree-climbing cukes. Now, I train cucumber vines on the fence. The sight of the long, green vegetables floating in mid-air unnerved some people.

Men on horseback used to work cattle in a meadow behind our neighborhood. Then, houses began to appear in the tall grass. The tall grass gave way to carpets of St. Augustine divided by bands of concrete. The meadow's creatures moved into the tops of live oak and water oak to watch for tiny movements in the grass. The owls' muted cries soothed children on the verge of sleep as every mouse in every house stayed wide awake.

The Mississippi River is a mile away. Some nights, I sit on the car listening to owl hoots and ship horns. It is the strangest love call you will ever hear.

When my glass is empty, I walk toward the house. At the door, the cat darts between my legs as the first bongs sound from the mantel. He's supposed to be an outside cat. Tonight, someone will find his bed shorter by about a foot.

Porch Steps
Baseball

Before organized sports ran the lives of families, you saw boys, and the occasional girl, facing their front porch steps in a pitcher's stance, shoulders squared, head down, one hand gripping a fuzzless tennis ball. If you were quiet and listened closely, you might hear The Voice.

I first heard The Voice the summer I was ten. The Voice, my voice trying to sound like the Chicago White Sox announcer, said, "Cullen has got to keep that fastball down or Mantle's going to park it in the center-field seats."

I sent the tennis ball crashing against the front porch steps. The Voice interpreted the ball's carom as hot grounder, line drive, pop up, or home run. The Voice praised good play and assigned error.

"Error on the second baseman. Runners at first and second. The pitcher rocks and fires."

From the pitcher's mound, I looked into the deep shade of the porch. Dark, screened windows flanked the front door. Flimsy white curtains billowed, pulled inside by an attic fan powerful enough to snatch small dogs from the lawn.

I cannot tell you how many times I took the measure of Mantle and Maris as thousands cheered and the curtains waved like pennants.

"MILL-dred!" (My grandmother calling to my mother.) "He's hitting the house with that ball again."

"Throw the ball *behind* the house," my mother, the peacemaker, would call from inside the dark recesses of the house.

"I'll be careful," I'd answer. "I won't hit the house."

Then, The Voice would pick up the action: "Cullen is under pressure from manager Al Lopez. He knows if one more fast ball sails on him, he's out of the game."

Of course, the next pitch *did* sail, smacking the wall between my grandmother's bedroom window and the front door. I didn't hang around for the manager's hook. I was around the corner of the house and down the driveway before my grandmother could come to her senses.

I hated the back porch steps. They were not a pitcher's steps. Too steep. Tennis balls came off the steps in flat, hard grounders that were hard to field. Every pitch was, as The Voice said, "an adventure."

With the decline of porches and steps, we don't see nearly enough kids talking to themselves on summer afternoons.

Every once in a while, I'll pick up a tennis ball a child has left lying in the grass, rock and fire the ball against the garden fence.

"Cowabonga! That guy's gotta be in his fifties."

And still bringing the heat, still hearing The Voice.

Hale-Bopp

The trip to The Farm had already reached a state of no-time before we left home.

At The Farm, there is nothing too inconsequential for me to ignore. One afternoon, I sat on the back porch of the little farmhouse built in the late 1940s to watch traffic on the big highway. Whoopee!

Then, I cracked open a can of ice cold Old Flugie. My neighbor, Ernie, gave me a six-pack as a going-away present. When I finished the beer, I threw the can into the yard as far as I could. Then, I reached for my pellet rifle and shot the unoffending beer can.

That's about as cerebral as it got for the next seven days.

I let the men and women who write for magazines do my thinking for me. I bought newspapers with my morning biscuit at the store up the road. The sign on the store's front door said, "No droopy pants." I hitched up and stepped inside.

The morning trip to the store on foot or by bicycle was my nod to exercise. I took long walks through the woods to the meadow and what people in these parts call a borrow pit. The dirt was "borrowed" for the U.S. highway that passes beyond one end of the pond. Most of the day, however, was spent reading on the long couch in the living room. Chilly afternoons, a small fire talked to itself behind a brick hearth.

The couch might have been built for giraffe surgery. Its width was generous, too. Small tables with lamps at either end, let two short people stretch out to read without their feet touching. I spent hours on the couch. I didn't read every story in the magazines or all of the books I took with me, but I read everything that interested me. Between naps.

My son came up at the end of the week to assume cooking duties. He likes to cook, and he's good at it. We have always encouraged him to do the things at which he excels. His mother turned the kitchen over without protest. I helped in my limited capacity of noncook. I made grits—from scratch—which took about a minute longer than instant, but tasted better.

I kept an eye on the chicken my son sautéed and put on a grill at the bottom of the back porch steps. This chore required that I lean over from a chair every ten minutes or so. That helped me work up an appetite.

My wife and I had passed idle hours playing dominoes on the dining room table. We introduced one of our son's friends to the game, but my son was holding out for a game of Hale-Bopp.

In 1997, finding the comet Hale-Bopp in the night sky was the thing to do. The comet had been discovered in the summer of 1995. Two years later, it was bright and easy to spot from a hill near the house.

About that time, my son and his uncle invented a game that called for throwing a ball of wound masking tape through the spaces where rafters lie across massive beams in the living room. One calls his shot, and if he makes it, the opponent must make the same shot or get a letter. A version of P-U-T-O-U-T and H-O-R-S-E, they called their game H-A-L-E-B-O-P-P.

It is a terrific way to kill oceans of time. It's not easy to throw the wad of tape through the gaps, but runs of luck or skill get the players revved up. People in the room, who are trying to ignore the game, rarely get revved unless the "ball," which is quite hard, bops them on the head.

I said a week at The Farm got no more cerebral than shooting beer cans with a pellet rifle. My son and I played two close games of Hale-Bopp. The hour was late and the games long. The second game, we shortened to B-O-P-P.

We drove three-quarters the length of Louisiana in the rain to get home. I awoke in my own bed the next morning to the first flashback to no-time.

Phoning Harry

Once, in a long telephone conversation, Harry told me that I must have insights into American life that he lacked. I worked for a newspaper. I saw behind the stage scenery.

I disagreed. I've always been the predictable one—working for a salary in the same town, at the same job, married to the same woman. Harry's a walking demographic. He climbed the corporate ladder, rode the cutting edge of technology, married, divorced, remarried.

Harry has the insights. Not me.

To be as different as two people can be in so many ways, we hold similar beliefs. His thinking is "Republican." I'm cast as the "Democrat." When we have finished yelling and kicking the camp chairs, we are high school friends and college roommates grown older.

When I'm camping with Harry, for that's how we invariably get together after long separations, I feel like I've just met Woody Allen at the Circle K and we've decided, just like that, to go camping. Harry looks like Woody Allen. When Harry and I hook up, it is usually to meet on a highway someplace and head for the woods.

We met in high school, though how we met is one of our favorite things to argue about. Skip that part. We were aware of each other's existence. One afternoon, we got together after school. He loved science fiction. I loathed it. He thought I was a snob. I thought he was a smart-ass. Two years later, we were college roommates.

If you could make two people with no common interests live together as college roommates, some semblance of friendship would result five times out of ten. This from research data I just made up.

If two young people happened to have a little in common, listened to each other's tales of woe, got drunk together, subsisted on pocket change, urged one another on in tough courses while learning to make $5 last two dates, those two people could be friends for life.

Despite our closeness, we made assumptions about each other. We attributed strengths to one another that neither of us had and from those imagined strengths drew real strength for ourselves. That's what we talk about when the fish aren't biting.

This time, I called Harry. "Leave your guns at home. Meet me at the place on U.S. 61. Don't be late."

He arrived three minutes late after a three-hour drive. "So I'm late. Sue me."

Harry likes guns. We grew up hunting on land where today a ruined shopping center hunkers. Harry likes well-made, expensive pistols, handguns with oomph. He talks about "stopping power" should bad guys creep up on him. In Harry's satire on the world, there are felons and space aliens hiding in the woods between his home in Mississippi and my place.

There was a candidate in a race for Louisiana governor Harry followed in the press. Harry liked what the guy had to say about guns. Harry lives in Mississippi. He wouldn't have voted for the guy, if he could. He just likes to hear people say nice things about guns.

On one camping trip, Harry shot our fire.

"No guns, right?" I said as Harry and I set up camp.

"Not a one," Harry chortled.

We both knew his pickup truck held enough firepower to tame the West, East, South, and North. There are places I camp where I like the idea of someone on my side packing heat. But when I got up in the night to go to the bathroom, I made lots of me-sounding noise. There was no sound of gunfire from Harry's tent that night, so I assumed he'd left his weapons in the truck or hadn't gotten to that part in his dreams where the space aliens come in.

Harry was up with first light, glancing over at me asleep under a mosquito bar. I squinched my eyes. I wanted to stay in bed another twenty minutes. Finally, he picked up his fly rod and addressed the indifferent fish in the lovely pond. A little while later, he moved off, and I slid out of my bag to make coffee.

We caught no more fish that morning than we had the previous afternoon, but we were relaxed and in no hurry to leave. We passed the morning and early afternoon talking. When we packed up and said our good-byes, it was as though we'd lived next door to each other the last twenty years. A year had passed since we last met. With promises to "do this again real soon and see you at my house if I don't see you at your house first," we drove out of the woods in separate trucks.

Months will pass before one of us picks up the telephone to resume a conservation that began when we were teenagers and continues into middle age.

October Best

Late October is the best time in South Louisiana. It's the payoff for surviving a summer that doesn't let up until the Halloween candy hits the store shelves.

October tells Louisiana school children that the calendar art in their classrooms was painted by someone who doesn't live here. My bank puts out a realistic calendar with photographs of swamp fishermen, Gulf Coast lighthouses, and plantation homes. I prefer the kind of calendar art I learned to love as a child — paintings of snowy Maine, Wisconsin in fall, Ohio at harvest time.

I love wearing tropical shirts and shorts to outdoor concerts in December, but let me mark the concert's date on a calendar where postmen's breath is visible and motorcycle cops look down red noses at small dogs.

Instead of first frost, fall in the South is often a case of first smell. Fragrances are some of my best memories of cool weather's arrival. The smell of juniper bushes at my grammar school would almost knock me down. My blue jeans returned fire with a powerful smell of their own.

Those jeans, purchased a week before school started, were stiff enough to nail up as storm shutters. Getting tackled hurt less the first weeks of school. Our jeans deflected the force of bony shoulders thrown at bony legs. Small children required parental help buttoning the unyielding fabric until Thanksgiving.

Yellow rain slickers worn by the fashionable student smelled like leftover linoleum. The plaid book satchels that made first-graders look like short door-to-door brush salesmen smelled of new Crayons, paste, wooden pencils, and rubber erasers.

October is the month I feel most alive. The air is cool and dry as straw. At night, traffic lights stand out like colored candle flames behind good crystal. Gone is summer. Gone the hot, wet air. Gone until June when barefoot boys in faded jeans appear on calendars to stare at fishing corks on water forever still.

That's a scene I know. It's a picture I want to cut out and frame to remind me on busy December days that if I work faster there'll be time to fish before dark.

First Fire

After the dinner hour, as the evening's first smoke curled from our chimney, there came a sharp rap at the front door. I opened the door to my neighbor, Jon, a good-looking lad who has lived next door since he was born. These days, I'm getting to know a new Jon, a boy on a high wire, balanced between childhood and manhood. He's thirteen—and a half.

Smoke or the promise of fire has always drawn Jon to our house. When he was little, it was his job to light the first fire of the season at our hearth. We would talk about where it was OK to start a fire and where it wasn't. I could have skipped the lecture, but we've always talked to Jon as though he were one of ours. Then, Jon, at my urging, would lay the long match he used to start the fire across adjacent logs, and we'd watch until the match caught fire, burned, and collapsed.

We'd make up a story about explorers escaping "The Valley of Fire."

Me: "Look, there goes the last guy; he's almost to the end of the suspension bridge." Jon: "The bridge is giving way. Oh, no. He jumps. Yes! He made it."

A couple of years ago, Jon missed the first fireside, but he lit the second fire of the winter. I was as enthusiastic as ever when our intrepid adventurers made their dash through "The Valley of Fire," but I sensed Jon was going through the motions—for my sake. The next winter, we didn't light a single blaze together. Alone in the living room, I provided the dialog at the collapse of the burning suspension bridge. "Who are you talking to?" my wife asked from the kitchen. "No one," I said.

Jon and I would meet in the street, I decompressing from a day at work, he taking a break from homework.

"I didn't light the first fire," Jon said.

"You haven't lit a fire this winter," I said.

"You want to light a fire, now?" he said.

"Maybe another night."

When I opened the door a few nights later to find Jon on the stoop, it was like old times. Then, he shattered the illusion with, "You wanna play chess?" Chess? We used to play checkers using plastic cowboy figures for black and Indian figures for red. (Kings were cowboys with guns drawn or Indians with war bonnets.) It wasn't just that Jon wanted to play a grownup's game. It was the way he stood under the porch lamp, a shoulder casually touching the doorframe, one leg crossed over the other. For a heartbeat, he was standing there in a blue paisley smoking jacket with black velvet lapels. I blinked him back to running shoes, T-shirt, and jeans.

"Come in," I said. We played one game before the long arm of Jon's mom reached out to snatch him back to homework. While we played, he'd told me he was doing well in school. He talked about wanting to go to college and his last soccer game. He explained inline skates to me. After he'd gone, I tried to remember that scary time between dweebhood and being old enough to get a driver's license. A girl once interrupted a monologue about myself on the telephone to tell me I'd said "man" twelve times in three minutes. I took it as a compliment.

Jon just skated by my front yard garden talking on a cordless telephone. Not a cell phone, a cordless phone, which means he can go only so far from his house before losing the connection. If I need to tell him something, like the time of the night's chess match, no problem. He has "call skating."

Velvet Purple
Coronet
Wind Thing

I'm bent double weeding thyme when what sounds like a rattlesnake starts up behind me. I jump and turn in one motion, heart hammering. The cognitive part of my brain knows there isn't a rattlesnake behind me. However, the part that controls jumping and screaming has the wheel at the moment.

When I land on my haunches and confront my attacker, I'm facing the velvet purple coronet wind thing that I bought one false spring day in January. Officially, it's The Velvet Purple Coronet Hummingbird, easily the gaudiest garden ornament allowed into the country by import regulations. It leaped into my hands from its perch beside the cash register at the hardware store where I'd gone to buy wood screws.

I bought the plastic bird (its wings are propellers) in anticipation of sun-filled spring days so lovely that people walk around bumping into things. "Look at that sky, the trees, the azaleas, feel the breeze—let me have a couple of those velvet purple coronet wind things, will you?"

That spring, my brother-in-law, son, and I convened in my bachelor brother-in-law's yard to garden. My son and I were in jeans and T-shirts. My brother-in-law, a lawyer, came to the garden in starched Oxford shirt, creased khaki trousers, and low-quarter hiking shoes, his concession to working in the dirt. He wields a trowel with the same elan he handles a notary's seal.

Before we were brothers-in-law, we were childhood friends. Add my son, a landscape architect, to the mix, and we are nitrogen, phosphorous, and potassium. We rarely agree on gardening decisions, but we work fast, often with hilarious results, ready to admit mistakes and re-do. My son, who once led his uncle and me on chases through woods and down creek sides, came willingly to his uncle's yard to play with us.

Brother-in-law and I paid close attention to the information on the plastic stick labels protruding from pots of transplants. We tried to remember proper spacing. We were doing well to consider height, color, and size at maturity. My son lectured us on design, "carrying the eye," and the cosmic ramifications of pansies planted too close to petunias which spread.

"Say, Junior, you're kneeling on the rosemary," said junior's uncle.

The day after the garden convocation, I found pieces of broken curbing near the lawyer's house. The pieces of concrete suggested a solution to the problem of lemon balm planted beneath a downspout. My brother-in-law was at his office. He would be there for hours. I was not sure the design would carry the eye. It might only work.

The Best Game
I Never
(Really) Played

I hear the crunch of car tires in gravel, inhale the smell of new-mown grass and overflowing garbage barrels, and my last summer of boys' baseball comes looping back.

We wore heavy, wool, buttoned jerseys in July, stirrup socks, and baggy pants little different from baseball uniforms of the nineteenth century. We itched. We were hot. We were cool.

The coach had been good enough to give me a chance to play even though I hadn't done well in tryouts. I don't know what possessed me to try out for Pony League, a league for teenagers who'd been playing ball since they were six.

The infielders moved like professionals. Without fear, they put their bodies in front of hard-hit grounders or dived to catch balls that I would have watched bounce past. The outfielders cruised the dark green lawn beyond the infield like ships-of-the-line. They tracked down fly balls on radar screens only they saw.

I didn't play much, which was fine with me. Batting was my introduction to panic attacks. I liked my seat in the dugout. There was nothing between me and the game, and only the most remote chance that I'd see duty.

On my rare trips to the plate in Little League, I knew the infielders on the other team were making the "swing-batter-batter" chant because I could see their mouths moving. My brain processed no sound. Fear effectively blocked all sensation save the small voice in my head that kept yelling, "Bail out!"

At the plate, I was in a world where time had stopped. I heard nothing of the noise in the bleachers behind me. The third-base coach, a man who spent the summer on the verge of apoplexy, was apparently mouthing instructions to me.

Then, his hands flew up in the semaphore of baseball, a code I enjoyed in the abstract when I was on the bench. But since my brain froze at the plate, he might as well have been waving, "Nice night for baseball." And it would have been if I hadn't been in the game.

People say of great hitters and fielders "they are in the zone." I, too, was in a zone—a zone ruled by the fear of getting hit in the head by a baseball. In Pony League, infielders didn't chant. That was kid stuff. No, they floated lightly over the dirt to vacuum up hot grounders. Then, they threw the ball to first base with accuracy and zip.

I didn't envy the players for whom the ballpark was a second home. I marveled at their ease on the dirt and grass. I knew some of the better players from school. A few of them were boys uncomfortable in class, but here under the lights they were straight "A" students of the line drive and the bunt. They were masters of picking up a curve ball as it left the pitcher's hand. They knew how to wait on it. Wait. Then, swing at the ball as though it hung before them in a spider's web.

I knew I was lucky to be on a team in Pony League and that this would be my last summer of baseball. The pitching was faster and better than my ability to hit it. I was in way over my head.

From my tryout in the advanced league, I had a new appreciation for first base. In games, the players with the long, thin gloves made it look easy. They stretched like ballet dancers, went into the dirt like back-hoes, or merely extended a glove to take the hard throw from shortstop.

On first base, I felt like the infielders knew I was a fraud and were punishing me by throwing the ball to me. It felt like they were throwing *at* me. I became a big fan of the starting shortstop whose throws were so on-line even I could catch them.

Why do I look back on that last summer of base-ball with such fondness? The fear has long since been replaced by the memory of the sound steel cleats made in gravel parking lots, the sound of boards creaking under the weight of the fans, and the smell of hot dogs rolling on their heated cylinders.

The same people I remembered from Little League were in charge of the hot dogs. The same voice called out the batter's name and the name of the player on deck. The same small boys played beneath the stands, pouring dirt into waxed Coke cups to compress the cups into crude baseballs.

The ball fields were near our little city's zoo. The crowd would get quiet as the pitcher went into his windup. Then, the monkeys would howl or a lion rock the night with a roar that seemed to come from Africa.

One afternoon this spring, I watched a high school shortstop field his position with confidence and grace. My eyes found another player who stood regarding the sky beyond the outfield fences. A fellow appreciator of the game, I thought, as the batter sent a ball flying at the setting sun.

Romancing the Nose

Before my wife, my mother was the woman I associated with a certain smell. I can't remember the name of her perfume, but it came in a glass bottle with a tiger skin cap. When I was six, I thought the tiny patch of tiger skin might be real.

One Mother's Day, I bought my mother the smallest bottle of tiger skin perfume made. It cost a fortune. On the way home from the drugstore on my bicycle, I hit a bump. The bottle of perfume rose from the bicycle's basket like an autumn moon. The bottle sailed up and over my head to shatter on the sidewalk. The scent of tiger skin perfume took on new meaning. It became the smell of disaster.

Shalimar was an untainted scent. It clung to a terry cloth shirt worn by the woman I would eventually marry. In the airport years, the smell of ashtrays, plastic lounge furniture, diesel fumes, jet fuel, rubber, hydraulic fluid, and people in a hurry competed with her smell. A few molecules of Shalimar would cling to me when the plane touched down on the other side of the country.

Shalimar gave way to a lotion she brought home from the hospital with the first baby, but the perfume's scent still makes me want to cuddle the bearer. I resist the temptation, the last one coming in an elevator crowded with elderly women.

There are scent epochs. The going-out-for-the-evening smell. The slaving-over-stove smell (Shalimar with a clove of garlic). The just-bathed smell. In the Shalimar days, I promised to care for her in sickness and in health. We assumed the health clause wouldn't be invoked until old age.

Bad backs—for each of us—proved the assumption wrong. These days, I react to a new scent. My wife had been out of town for a few days when a woman at the office passed close by my desk. My pulse quickened. I breathed deeply to inhale the aphrodisiac of "Deep Cold Therapeutic Mineral Ice."

Hamsters

I picked up pieces of fragrant cedar that had fallen under the assault of a ground crew's chain saws. The heady smell of the wood transported me to a shed reeking of hamsters and cedar shavings.

The air was crisp and newly fall. I wasn't ten, yet. Sycamore leaves the size of national flags lay upon the ground. When I walked on the leaves to the shed that smelled of cedar shavings, the noise was almost deafening.

The hamsters that lived in the shed heard me coming. The small, furry mammals were unwilling subjects in my Great Failed Hamster Breeding Project. *Crunch, Crunch, Crunch* went the leaves under ankle-choking canvas basketball shoes.

Inside the shed, profound ignorance rubbed shoulders with unbounded enthusiasm. The hamsters, grown fat on their keeper's exuberant feeding schedule and secure in their oft-changed cedar shavings, lived a great life.

Me, I was pretty happy, too. I was in love with a girl named Rita. Junior high school stuff. There was about as much danger of my getting in over my head with Rita as there was of the hamsters mating. In fact, there was no chance whatsoever of the pig-eyed, furballs mating because they were the same sex, though I was never able to determine *which* sex.

If I'd worked in the labs at Los Alamos, I'd have glowed like a neon beer sign. The FBI would not have believed anyone could be *that* dumb. To them, my lab would have smelled not of cedar shavings but conspiracy. I don't remember the name of the, uh, male hamster, but I called the, uh, girl hamster Rita. How proud the woman of my unacknowledged love would have been to know that I'd named a rat after her. And that I was trying to breed the rat to another rat of the same sex.

I had gotten into hamster breeding to impress Rita. I could see the headline in *My Weekly Reader* — "Louisiana youth corners hamster market; Pet shops line up at door of backyard breeding shed."

I imagined leaving town on business trips with a ventilated suitcase filled with tiny, red, hairless hamsters. (I'd have hired a kid to finish junior high school for me.) I reckoned I had as good a chance of getting the breeding pair right as I did getting it wrong. Rita could have easily been a Rex.

The how-to book made it sound so easy. "Gently lift a hamster into the air. Carefully roll it over in the palm of your hand and look for either an 'exclamation point' or a 'comma.'"

If I'd succeeded in increasing the size of my breeding herd, you can bet the first things I'd have bought from profits would have been a white lab jacket and a magnifying glass.

"So what are they — male or female?"

My little sister. Always in the way. Always asking the questions I should have asked before the neighbors called the cops.

"Come on, which is it, exclamation point or comma?"

"Gee, I don't know," I'd say. "Sort of a question mark or maybe a semicolon, if I had to guess."

And into the breeding box the hamsters would go for the prescribed number of days. Then, I'd separate the indifferent lovers for the number of days recommended by the book. I renewed the library book on hamster breeding eighteen times. Looking back, the breeding pair, Rita and what's-its-name, acted more like best pals than seductress and bull hamster.

The supplier of my breeding pair was a kid who knew as much about hamsters as I did. He'd just lucked out in the mating department, got an exclamation point in the ol' breeding cage with a comma at just the right time. Then, he lucked out again when the mom hamster didn't eat her babies and his profits.

I never got any hamsters to mate. I went into journalism instead of biology and spared some genetics lab an enormous lawsuit.

Who Is What They Used to Be?

"Southerners Not What They Used to Be," read the headline on the first story in a six-page layout of Associated Press reports on the changing South. Southerners aren't what they used to be? Well, Lawd, chile, who is? Why, many Southerners of my acquaintance, especially ones from my childhood, aren't even still among the quick.

I love it when writers and reporters stumble upon the South. We are only sometimes found to be dangerous, illiterate, or racist, but always not what we used to be. These six newspaper pages of breathstopping reporting could easily have been about the West, the Northwest, the Midwest, Down East, Eastern Seaboard, or the Middle East. The Middle East is forever not being what it used to be.

The AP's discovery of a changed South appeared in a Friday paper. There should be a rule of journalism that this many words on the same subject run only on Sunday. This reportage required nappage. I tore out the pages and stuffed them into the bag where I put things to be read later but soon. This morning, I spread the pages across my desk and went to reading—yellow highlighter darting to lines like this one: "The South has become sort of like a lifestyle, rather than an identity anymore."

Whew! Grammar has become sort of like something people once knew.

Sort of like a lifestyle, eh? Just kinda slip into being Southern the way you would a surfer's wet suit, a skier's boots, or a NASCAR fan's patch jacket. Once you'd tucked the South into the tops of your work boots, what would you be styling—a banker, university professor, cross burner, woman neurosurgeon, male nurse, or proprietor of one of North Carolina's last country stores?

The latter would be Vernon Yates of Cary, N.C., owner of Yates Grocery and Farm Supply. The store sells neither groceries nor farm supplies. The AP doesn't tell us what, if anything, is sold there. The store stocks such Yatesisms as, "Everything is completely different from what it used to be." Yes, Yates, who is almost seventy, has seen change. Cary, N.C., the local wags like to say, stands for "Containment Area for Relocated Yankees."

These six pages of words try to assert that if there ever was a South, as opposed to a Louisiana or a Mississippi or a North Carolina or a Tennessee, the region owed its charms or horrors to a whole lot of its being countryside. I'm a Southerner who grew up next door to a man who played the guitar on his front porch, across the street from a synagogue. On the other side of him, a Baptist lady taught classical piano. As I delivered the newspaper on my bicycle, all sorts of anomalies leapt from the azalea bushes. There were men born and reared Southerners who fought in World War I, World War II or Korea, and hated war. The Associated Press stories on the changed South say the armed forces are full of Southerners, deeply patriotic descendants of people who fought to leave the Union. It's possible, the stories allow, that many Southerners join the military because they've been squeezed out of work by big companies that hire foreigners. How this is different from being squeezed in

North Dakota isn't clear. Black people call themselves Southerners, the Associated Press discovered. Well, the AP has been around since 1848. Not much escapes the wire services' notice.

I got carried away with my highlighting, underlining stuff in ballpoint pen, bracketing entire paragraphs in blue wax pencil, and making smudges with a pencil lead the size of a fishing line sinker. Then, the voices of Gibbs and Yvonne rose above the sound of furious highlighting.

Gibbs and Yvonne covered courts for my newspaper, banging out their stories over a running conversation about their grandmothers. Gibbs was middle-aged and white. Yvonne was in her late twenties and black. When Gibbs occasionally used a word to describe her people that Yvonne felt inappropriate, she'd say, voice rising on the short "i"—"Gibbs!" "Oh, sorry," Gibbs would say and rush on with whatever he was saying about the district court judges. Gibbs and Yvonne respected each other. At Gibbs' funeral, Yvonne couldn't stop crying. What they'd found in common were their grandmothers who used the same rural expressions and cooked the same Upland South food.

If there's something changing in America, it isn't lifestyles. We all practice some form of the same vague idea of the good life—or try. What's changing is land that once supported woods. Grass and crops are filling up with houses competing for the most square footage outside Parliament and the Taj Mahal. The people who live in these houses may be sons or daughters of the South, or they may be corporate transfers from Illinois. If they draw nothing from the land around them or the people or the people's history, it doesn't matter what they call themselves. If they're slaves to work and captives of television, computers, and electronic games, and you must call them something, call them clueless when it comes to where they live.

Driver's Ed

In high school driver's ed class, coaches and students meet as equals. Coaches have the authority implied by silver-plated whistles and clipboards. Students have their hands on the steering wheels of powerful machines, a fact that isn't lost on their instructors.

The coach who taught me driver's education was also my world history teacher. He asked, "Who were the Axis Powers?" in the same alarmingly shrill voice he used when giving the VD lecture in health class or telling us to take another lap in track practice.

"What was the Maginot Line, nimrod?" he'd bark at a half asleep student. "The sum of the squares of the other two sides?" ventured dim Nimrod.

"I'll see you in gym class, funny man."

There was always the punishment of gym class awaiting comedians in Coach's academic classes. You could needle Coach, but it was you who felt the pain.

Now, the voice said, "All right, let the clutch out — slowly, this time."

Saturday mornings in driver's ed, Coach was at the mercy of the students he'd called idiots and MO-rons earlier in the week. We were student drivers. We didn't know what we were doing. That's why we were in driver's ed. So, if we hit the brakes a little too hard or popped the clutch while depressing the accelerator, we were blameless.

With practice, we learned to watch Coach's head from the corners of our passenger-side eyes. Hit the brakes, and his head shot forward. Stomp the gas while popping the clutch, and his head snapped back.

"Let me try that again, Coach. Hold on."

Learning manual transmission in city traffic was bad enough. Parallel parking was torture. Parallel parking between cars in the gym parking lot was something half the driver's ed students would simply never get.

"Try it again," Coach said.

"Coach, really, I just can't . . ."

"Can't?" Coach sneered. "I didn't hear you say *can't*, did I? There's no *can't* in this car."

I used to wonder who owned the cars we attempted to park between. Why would anyone subject his automobile to repeated ramming by students attempting to parallel park? The cars might have belonged to people Coach didn't like. Maybe they owed him money.

There was a written test in driver's ed, but the real final exam was rolling up an incline, holding the car with brake, clutch and gas, and pulling onto a busy highway.

We accomplished the feat by launching our big Ford passenger cars—and their occupants—as though from a pad at Cape Canaveral. We drove three to a car—driver, coach, and student in the back seat awaiting his or her turn in the hot seat. You and the kid in the back seat knew what was coming. You held your breath and enjoyed the thrill of imminent death. Coach's scream seemed to come from a place far away.

The coaches who lasted three summers of driver's ed were placed on fast track for assistant principal. The casualties became shot put coaches and taught shop. Shop students knew the coaches were broken men. We finished them off by gluing the tool cabinet shut.

Bobby's Gun

A small voice had been telling me to get rid of the shotgun and rifle in my house. I had not fired the shotgun since boyhood. The rifle, an unwanted gift of a friend, I had never fired.

For years, the shotgun had leaned, sturdy, oiled, heavy in a corner of my closet. Though I hadn't had shells for it in many years, I would take it out from time to time to swing and sight, pretending to pull the trigger on imaginary squirrels in the hall outside my bedroom.

This was my cousin Bobby's shotgun. After he'd grown to be a man and left home, his father—my Uncle Bob—presented the shotgun to me the first (and only) time he took me deer hunting.

I suppose Bobby knew his father had given me the 20-gauge. It wasn't expensive. It came from Sears, held five shells, plugged to hold the legal three. Hunting squirrel or deer, you got one good shot because the shotgun was bolt action.

I didn't hunt much of anything. Before I went to live with my Uncle Bob and Aunt Aggie, all I hunted were hapless turtles and snakes with a Daisy air rifle and, then, only if I could get my Uncle Bill to take me into the country. Suddenly, I was in the big leagues. Men were thrusting shotguns and high-powered rifles at me, urging me to rise before the sun to kill something.

I tell you what I liked most about that hunting camp. I liked the warmth of the potbellied stove and the smell of blue smoke that leaked into the room. I liked the biscuits, eggs, and sausages cooked by one of the men who worked with my uncle at the feed and seed store. I liked the coffee that slammed you into wakefulness. Mine had milk in it. Most of all, I liked sticking my nose out from the pile of covers that lay between me and the hunting shack's predawn freezing air.

When I left camp to hunt, it was with reluctance. My Uncle Bob knew this. He gave me a puny shotgun (though loaded with shells he called bear balls) just in case a deer came after the Fig Newtons in the pockets of my hunting jacket. The only way I was going to shoot a deer was in self-defense.

One morning, I saw a buck, big and beautiful, standing in a small clearing planted in rye grass. I regarded the deer as though it were in a painting, as I reached for the apple inside the pristine blood pouch in the back of my jacket. Teeth biting into apple made a sound like an explosion (a juicy one, too) in the deathly still woods. Uncle Bob, unknown to me, had the big buck in his sights when I detonated the fruit.

My uncle wasn't happy. I regretted chomping on the apple, but that didn't keep me from clamping my teeth on a Butterfinger scarcely fifteen minutes later. The other hunters were alert, poised, ready to deal death from their stands. I was determined that no snack in the ample pockets of my jacket would make it back to camp.

It was cold. The freezing air hurt my fingers and made my nose run. I didn't thaw until I was driving home with Bobby, in a warm car, sleeping, waking, sleeping.

Bobby, beloved cousin and big brother, died this winter. At his funeral, I told his son, Robert, that the shotgun was his. This summer, before the opening of fall deer season, I gave the gun to its rightful owner. Bobby's son marveled at the old shotgun. He listened as I told of my one trip to hunting camp with his dad, someone I think about a lot, especially in the fall when a man's thoughts turn, inexorably, to cold woods and candy bars.

Amal Is Back

Amal, the night visitor, is back. Amal. That's what I've taken to calling the armadillo that visits my garden on cool fall nights. Amal is looking not for a miracle but for grubs that glow enticingly in the light of the street lamp next to my front yard garden.

This tank of an animal, this throwback to a time when an armadillo's biggest threat was not car tires but any animal able to flip it and eat it, comes around a few nights after I've turned the dirt to plant mustard seed and transplant red sail lettuce.

I don't know where Amal lives, but I suspect under a neighbor's shed, beneath houses that are on piers, and, possibly, the drainage culvert that runs beside my garden. I do know this: Amal has the timing of a U.S. Navy seal on a mission of do-or-die.

This armadillo is clever, though his head, so tiny compared to the rest of him, doesn't seem large enough to hold a long thought. Amal doesn't dig in undisturbed ground. He roots in the ground that I've busted, pulverized with a hoe, fluffed with a garden fork, and decorated with tender plants.

He's after the grubs. Make no mistake. In the morning, when I approach the garden with a steaming cup of coffee and the hope born of sunrise, I find a garden that looks like it's been churned by an outboard motor's propeller. In Amal's wake, my red sail leaf lettuce lies atop the ground like debris from a party barge.

What's this that greets my morning eyes? Has gravity been turned off during the night? Has a playful neighbor on his third Old Flugie played a prank? No, surely, it's an animal, but what animal has been so careful in its destruction, so thoughtful in its cultivation?

A cat? Doubtful. Cats never work long enough at a stretch to cause so much turned earth. A dog? Hardly. If this were the work of a dog, there'd be a single trough of a hole with a nearby hill of dirt.

The first time Amal came, I replanted the uprooted vegetables the morning of discovery and was lying in bed the next night wondering what had been in the garden and if it would return. Then, outside the window I heard the slow shuffling of the armadillo, like a Depression-era hobo, noisily shoving aside empty plastic plant pots, rolls of chicken wire, and the summer's tomato stakes.

I have a neighbor who does more damage in my garden than Amal. This guy has a knack for stepping on everything between the entrance to the garden and the basil he craves. I rearranged plants in the garden so that the interloper could harvest herbs for that night's dinner without flattening everything in his path.

By comparison, Amal is considerate. He doesn't eat the lettuce. He lifts and separates it from the dirt in search of grubs. Usually, it's not hard to replant the lettuce or the parsley or the green onions. Sometimes, after one visit, Amal doesn't return. He knows the thoroughly worked plot has yielded its grubs.

I've tried spreading blood meal and red pepper. The last time, I swear I heard Amal yell, "Aieee, laissez le bon temps roule!" (Let the good times roll!) as he rolled out of sight.

That's the thing about gardening in South Louisiana. Everybody likes his food spicy.

Thunder Happy

The sound that thunder makes has always seemed friendly to me. If not friendly, then reassuring. The sky would boom, and I'd tell myself, "Thunder doesn't hurt you." Now, lightning . . .

I was past forty before anyone I knew was struck by lightning. I'd read about fishermen and ballplayers getting hit by lightning. A book called *1001 Questions Answered about the Weather* told me 500 people a year are killed by lightning in the United States and that 2,000 people are injured.

The person I knew who was struck by lightning worked at the newspaper. He was walking up the front drive when WHAM! I saw him after the ambulance had arrived and he'd been loaded onto a gurney. He looked surprised, and his hair was sproingy.

Now, when that reporter's name comes up in conversation, someone always says, "He's the guy who got hit by lightning." Being struck by lighting has become a distinction the man will carry with him the rest of his life.

Because I've never been struck by lightning, it remains an abstraction. Thunder seems more real. Listening to a thunderstorm from a warm, dry bed is one of life's great pleasures. Electronics and computers are marvelous, but roof and walls remain two of mankind's greatest achievements.

I grew up in the time just before the television set became a household fixture. It was a good time, for which I'm increasingly nostalgic. People talked to one another in the long evenings. They read newspapers and books. They sat on front porches and talked to people walking by.

Before the universal sound blanket of television (and air conditioning), people raised their windows in the summer time. Snatches of conversation and the smell of people's suppers drifted through the houses. Now, we're sealed inside our houses like larvae.

Thunder takes us by surprise. It wakes us up to the outside world. In the long ago, the weather was entertainment. On summer afternoons, we watched for an hour as a thunderstorm pulled itself together. We listened as the thunder rumbled closer, the smell of rain in the air. It was disappointing if the rain didn't come.

The weather station of my childhood was a cement porch. The surface was as smooth as an ice cube and, next to a bare belly, almost as cool. There wasn't a better place for watching thunderstorms build over Vance Avenue. And when the rain finally did come, it was wild. Rain fell like molten lead, pounding the sidewalk, shaking the leaves and limbs on the crape myrtle at the end of the porch. My pals and I lay as still as seals to watch the rain come down.

The afternoon rain offered the only break in the heat unless you paid a dime to be admitted to the air-conditioned darkness of the Don Theater. At the Don, we watched Tarzan sleep on a mat of woven leaves. He looked cool, asleep in the steamy jungle. For one thing, he wasn't wearing pajamas, nor was he wrapped in moist bed sheets. When the serials, feature film, and cartoons were over, the ushers at the Don would throw open the doors for us to go slit-eyed into the glare and heat of late morning. The highlight of the day was over, unless after-noon brought a good thunderstorm.

It took me awhile to realize that things that cost money don't bring happiness of themselves. Friendship, marriage, children showed me the contentment sharing affords. The first thunderstorm my grandson and I shared we were talking in the shed as rain pounded the tin roof. We took inventory of every tool that hung from a nail as thunder boomed far away, then closer, then right on top of us.

Those High Flying Tree Guys

I was in the kitchen the morning The Tree Guys shifted into high gear. I walked to the window and froze. Sections of water oak the size of drain culverts were falling six stories to hit the ground with the impact of meteorites. Chain saws screamed banshee love calls. A rope weighted by a man swung between tree limbs. It was horrifying and riveting.

I felt like a four-year-old watching heavy construction for the first time. Carpenters working on a house just out of range of the arboreal atomic bombs stopped to watch. The carpenters held their knuckles against their teeth as they watched sawdust rain down through a white mist of testosterone. There were moments when it took everything I had to keep watching, like when a Tree Guy hung by a rope to saw off the limb he was standing on.

The day before, my wife had called me at work. "You should see this! There is an entire tree (a limb the size of a tree) swinging over the yard."

"Get out of the house!" I screamed.

"Not *our* yard, the yard where the tree is—was." This last was punctuated by what sounded like a bank vault hitting the ground.

The Tree Guys took down two huge water oaks and a pecan while yelling to one another in the language of men who do dangerous, exhilarating work.

"Moan back with da truh." (Come on back with the truck.)

This was a low-budget job. One of The Tree Guys would stick his head out of the cab of his truck to make "Beep, Beep" sounds as he backed up. The Other Tree Guys slapped their chaps in glee and called "Moan back" some more.

"Own me, now. Own me." (On me. I've taken up the slack in the rope and will maintain tension until you come flying off that tree, chain saw biting thin air.)

"Take a 90 on that rope." (If you don't wrap your end of the rope around something solid, like another tree, that two-ton limb is going to yank both your arms off.)

"Quick, set that fence back up." (No translation necessary.)

A borrowed hydraulic wood splitter arrived, along with primitive gleaners who'd heard the chain saw's mating call and answered. Loading split wood into a pickup truck, I thought of the time I almost offed my Aunt Aggie.

My aunt, a wisp of a girl in her late seventies, was watching me split wood in a neighbor's backyard. I'd settled her into an aluminum folding chair near the right back tire of my old blue pickup truck. We were having a fine time when I tossed one too many pieces of split wood into the truck bed. The exploding truck tire rocked Aunt Aggie in her light chair, straightened her curly hair, and placed a look of surprise on her face that lingered for days. We laugh about it now, especially when she starts shrieking at the sight of tires, trucks, trees, or anything blue.

Like many Baton Rouge neighborhoods, we have a lot of old water oaks that are starting to come down — on their own or at the hands of The Tree Guys. I hate it when homeowners cut down trees when a good trimming is called for. Take out the trees, and you give a street that "air base look."

Storms give my neighbors and me enough firewood to get us through nuclear winter. What we don't burn in fireplaces, we burn in chimineas. Warming ourselves in the cherry glow of the little patio stoves, we talk of hurricanes, crashing limbs, and the thrilling aerial exhibit provided by The Tree Guys.

Winter Cyclists

Girls on new bicycles approach in late afternoon winter light. The riders are oblivious to the pale wash of blue sky, cool air, and patches of still-green grass. The girls are fixed on the gear shifters inside the handlebar grips on their Christmas bikes.

"I'm in gears 3 and 7," a rider says.

"Try 1 and 4," says the girl on her wingtip. "That's where I am."

The bicyclists glide by as I turn compost and dirt into beds for romaine lettuce, arugula, and mustard greens. I pause to listen to the cockpit chatter.

The girls cruise in squadrons of three or four. Children on the verge of young womanhood, they are beyond the pull of parental gravity when they ride bicycles. They have graduated from piloting machines with foot brakes and one gear to mountain bikes with cantilevered brakes controlled by hand and twenty-one speeds.

That's twenty more speeds than bicycle riders in Baton Rouge need.

There are no hills in Baton Rouge, only small rises from land to higher land. At thirty feet above sea level, increased pedal pressure conquers most elevations. The riders passing my front yard garden are feminine Chuck Yeagers, girls drawling that test pilot talk.

"Try 2 and 4."

"Four's too easy. Go to 6."

The girls move by, their wrists sending messages to derailleurs, chains slackening to tighten again in new configurations. My shovel's blade exposes white grubs to the buttery sun as I follow the girls' progress down our dead-end street.

A few minutes later, back they come. The girls are riding faster now. They've found just the right gears. Up the street they go, leaning into the wind, hair flying, ears tuned to a private frequency.

They are free—until suppertime.

Convenience Stores Offer Look at Culture

I've come to think of convenience stores as The Gasoline Store of Hopes and Dreams. "Store" is singular since the insides are hard to distinguish from each other and the same conversation runs nonstop in each place. Eavesdrop on a conversation between two people looking for work and hear the conclusion of the chat at another store—between two other people—as you pay for coffee that tastes pre-Hurricane Katrina.

These little plastic and tin temples of Hopes and Dreams are presided over by insanely cheerful foreigners, or dour persons from other countries, or lively black women who range in age from early 20s to mid-60s.

In these Egalitarian Gasoline Dispensaries, a customer and the person behind the counter could exchange places and never miss a beat. To a customer complaining about the rise and fall of the price of gasoline (as it continues to rise): "Honey, I know it. I get my gas from the same pumps and, no, I don't get a discount, either."

There are sociologists hard at work in windowless rooms trying to prove that poverty, homelessness, and unemployment color one's view. They need to get out more. I suggest they line up to buy a Powerball ticket. That takes a while. And keep their recorders running.

"Did you check out that job?" a clerk asked the young man in front of me. The young man was holding a cold six-pack of cheap, light beer as though he didn't mean to fumble. "Yeah, I looked into it," he said. "Pays the same as what I'm doing." The clerks hear things as they stab cash register keys, flip gasoline pump switches, direct the swiping of credit cards, and crank out lottery tickets. They pass the information along to their customers, taking their clues from the little things people say as they plunk down their purchases on rubber change mats.

Another young man puts down four cans of beer held together by circles of plastic and two cans he found loose in the case. "Bless you," the clerk says. "I hate it when people bust up a six pack to get two beers." Not only will researchers get valuable first-hand information waiting in line, some of them will eventually win big money, taking some of the pressure off government funding of obvious conclusions.

The country stores of today are places where wisdom is dispensed not by straw-sucking men in overalls but young women with their bellies showing. Just when I'm about to swear off reading the newspaper or ask my wife to cut out the stories about government waste and senseless wars, I stand in line waiting to pay for off-brand milk and hear a college student say something so utterly optimistic I want to hug him. "Hold that thought," I want to say. "Hold it with all your might." One day, that student will graduate, get a job, and shop at a better class of store—one that sells clothing or groceries or liquor but not gasoline. And those stores are fine. What they lack is customer diversity and varying degrees of hopefulness and despair.

Forget cultural diversity. This is America. The culture is automatically diverse. Promote diversity of opinion and experience. And when you hear it, listen. If you win the lottery, don't forget where the ticket came from. And if you drink, do so responsibly.

The Visitor

One Saturday afternoon, my wife answered a knock at the door to find a young man standing on the porch. She stepped outside, and I returned to my take-out dinner and a movie.

A few minutes had passed when my wife and the visitor walked by the window. Our caller held a disposable camera in one hand.

"Is there still an oak tree in the back yard?" I heard him ask.

I didn't know who he was, but I knew why he'd come.

A few more minutes had gone by when my wife and the visitor walked into the house. "This is Sean," my wife said. "He used to live in our house."

Sean was in his thirties. He was a small child when his father, a math professor, and mother bought the house. Sean had come to see how his old house compared to his memories.

Sean's family moved to another state years ago, but while they lived in this house, Sean's dad had planted a small live oak. Baton Rouge is a city of grand, sprawling live oak trees. There is an oak in our neighborhood that began to grow before the American Revolution.

The tree Sean's father planted is small by live oak standards. We told Sean, apologetically, that his tree would be bigger but for the canopy of other trees that shelter our—his—house from the sun. I'd known Sean five minutes. He felt like part of the family.

Sean's work took him around the country. "I'm doing a job in New Orleans," he told us. "This close to Baton Rouge, I knew I had to get a picture of my dad's tree."

After Sean had taken his picture of the live oak, my wife took a picture of him standing beneath the tree.

"It was this big when my dad planted it," Sean said. The little tree probably wasn't as thick as the index finger Sean held up.

We were impressed by Sean's sense of mission. He told us his mother had died. His sister, Sean said, had stood in our street a few years ago to glimpse her father's oak rising behind our house. Now, Sean had a picture to show their dad.

Watching Sean drive away, I knew the first house I'd visit on a tour of old home places. It would be the duplex where I built Erector Set Ferris Wheels on a screened porch on afternoons when it rained, the house where my French grandmother lit holy candles in blood red jars to save us from lightning strikes.

We are drawn to our old houses hoping to find at least one thing that is the way we left it. We may hope to hear the voices that once warmed the walls. Failing that, it is enough to have gone home.

Cat People

Here I am in the cat supplies aisle at 9:30 at night looking for food, kitty litter, and flea drops. Earlier in the day, my wife and I had said we'd take a homeless cat living at our son's house in Lafayette. Faster than you can say I-10 Swamp Expressway, there was a knock at our door. I opened the door and my son, smiling, walked through with our new cat—Lillie.

Of course, we didn't know the cat's name when we met her. She was a homeless cat who'd been living beneath an azalea bush. How fast things change in the life of a cat and her human family. It took us a couple of days to name the cat. My wife got the honor. The kitty box is in her bathroom. I consider that a fair swap. From sleeping under an azalea bush, Lillie has gone to sleeping pretty much wherever she wishes. Not only does she sleep where she wishes, she is praised lavishly for her good choices. "Oh, look where Lillie's sleeping now. In the middle of our bed. Get the camera."

I may no longer laugh at middle-aged men and women who've turned their lives over to exceedingly small, brown dogs with pointed ears. We are now one of those couples, only our dog is a cat.

We've always been a cat family. Before the enlightenment, our neighborhood was like most others. Cats roamed the streets, yowling as they mated under houses and producing in short order—kittens. We raised our share of neighborhood cats. We got them fixed. Got their shots and gave them names.

In the early days, the children named the cats, which explains names like "Homely," "Scat Cat," and "Oddibe." I could never keep the names straight, but the children on the street and their mothers referred to the cats as though they were neighbors who ate from bowls and licked themselves clean.

Animals are part of childhood. The deaths of pets are often children's introduction to mortality and grave-side services. I've buried a couple of cats, tears streaming down my cheeks as I thought about their time in our lives. One cat's life spanned the end of our children's grammar-school years to their college years. After that cat died, we needed some time before the next one.

This cat will be an inside cat. This cat already is an inside cat. "Is it all right with you if I clean off the top of the bookshelves in the spare bedroom so Lillie can look out the window?" my wife asked. "Great idea," I said, as though I'd just been asked, "Is it okay with you if I put our money in a sure-fire mutual fund?"

We share our homes with animals—once we've decided to share our homes with animals—the way we accommodate small children and elderly parents. A learned cat scholar writes that cats adopt humans rather than the other way around. Cats make us part of their families. Cats can't move furniture. So, we do the heavy lifting. But it's the cat's idea.

I got home the other night as proud of my cat purchases as I was with formula for our first child. In a moment, I'll return to handcrafting an adorable toy for Lillie made of string, Christmas ribbon, and a cardboard tube. I have nothing better to do. Really. I have nothing better to do.

Chilling During Surgery

I was feeling a little stressed the other morning. A doctor was about to stick an extremely sharp object — a knife of sorts — into my eye in an operation he called strictly routine. Strictly routine is when a doctor sticks a knife in someone else's eye. If it had been up to me, I would have been gassed but good and never known anything about what the doctor was doing in my eye. But that's not the way they do these strictly routine operations.

A nurse gives you a shot to relax you. If I want to relax, I go fishing. If someone's about to stick sharp metal in my eye, I want something to knock me out. I'd had this strictly routine operation on my other eye. So, I knew the doctor was going to shine a very bright light in my eye for the thirty minutes it took to remove a cataract-clouded lens and replace it with a clear, artificial lens. I knew the surgeon was going to talk to me the whole time, too. You know, make chit-chat, because that's what he did the last time.

Now that I'm older than most of my doctors, I feel free to address them as though they were a son or daughter. "Would this go any quicker if we didn't talk?" I asked during the first operation. "Not really," the doctor said. So, I tried a relaxation technique that usually works for me as long as there's no pain involved. I tried to imagine a beach in warm sunshine or walking through a high, cool forest or falling asleep to the sound of rain on the roof. But all I could see was this guy dressed like a pack of Winston cigarettes.

I knew the guy. He was real. He'd laughed at me before Christmas as I walked through the atrium of the gambling boat/hotel downtown. He was dressed like a pack of cigarettes and he laughed at me because I was wearing bicycle clothes that didn't match. By international agreement, bicycle shirts, pants, socks, shoes, helmet, gloves are not allowed to match. If we look like children dressed by mothers on acid when we're *on* our bicycles, we are truly bizarre looking when our bicycles are nowhere in sight.

This guy dressed like a pack of Winston cigarettes leaned over to tell a fellow employee, "Check out this dude." I couldn't hear what he said. I read it in the way his chest and belly were heaving with laughter. Funny thing. It struck me hilarious, too, and I started laughing. Here's a gambling boat/hotel employee who's allowed to wear NASCAR clothing to work and he's laughing at the way *I'm* dressed.

Then, it occurred to me that Winston might not sponsor race cars anymore because, you know, NASCAR is hip and cool and smoking isn't. That means the guy dressed like a pack of Winston cigarettes had put the ensemble together himself. "Honey, where are my red pants? I want to wear them with my red-and-white checked shirt, white shoes, and red cap."

I, of course, had dressed *myself* mostly for warmth but not without an eye to style—long blue tights under shorter bicycle shorts, high-tech jersey with deep pockets in the small of the back, socks of at least three colors, and shoes of two colors. Did I say the jersey was covered with fire breathing lizard-frogs? It was—and is.

132

That was the best relaxation scenario I could come up with—a guy dressed like a pack of cigarettes, laughing at me. I asked the surgeon to tell me about the operation before mine and to spare no details. Both operations turned out fine.

Christmas Calling

As fondly as I hold the memories of my children's Christmases, it is not any of those Christmases that come to mind in the last moments before sleep on December nights. One evening, as a friend and I neared the end of a walk, I asked her what first came to mind when she thought of Christmas.

"Tangerines and chocolate Kisses," she said.

When my friend, Mary, was little, her mother brought a stocking filled with, among other things, tangerines and chocolate Kisses to her bed on Christmas morning. Mary imagines her father building a fire in the living room or attending to some last minute detail as she spilled the contents of the stocking onto the bed covers.

Now, in early middle age, she recalled that first taste of tangerine slices and chocolate Kisses. I almost had the taste and the feeling of the fruit's roughness and the smell of the orange skin. The tips of my fingers tingled with the tactile memory of unwrapping the wrinkled foil skin of a chocolate Kiss.

"My mother brought me tangerines and chocolate Kisses on Christmas morning even after I had children," Mary said. "She brought them to me every Christmas, almost until the year she died."

If we'd had another block or two to walk, I might have told Mary about the heavy cardboard box that appeared beneath our tree on Christmas Eve when I was nine. I had memorized the appearance and position of every gift under the tree. I spotted the box as I walked into the living room and saw the presents half-hidden by the Scotch pine's fragrant branches.

Turning to my father at the dining room table, I said, "There's a shortwave radio in that box, isn't there?"

I was in love with the idea of "tuning in the world on shortwave radio." Those very words appeared in an ad in the back of one of my comic books.

I knew about long distance radio listening. I'd taken to falling asleep with the earpiece of a crystal radio jammed into the left side of my head. One winter night, the sounds of the Grand Ol' Opry, hundreds of miles from the head of my bed, had ridden the crystal cold airwaves down the skies and into my skull. I was sure the plain cardboard box, taped closed against prying eyes and fingers, held a shortwave set much like the one I'd seen a German spy using in a movie at the Don Theater on Bolton Avenue.

"It's a shortwave radio, isn't it?" I said again.

My father looked at me as though I were a talking cat.

"It's *not* a shortwave radio," he said. "It's jelly."

He turned to my mother, "Why does he think there's a shortwave radio in that box?"

"Because he wants it to be," my mother said.

"All right, it's a shortwave radio," my father said.

Oh, joy. A shortwave radio!

Hurry, Christmas Eve, and be over. Let it be morning. In the briefest interval between conscious thought and sleep, I heard Radio Netherlands calling through the whistling and crackling of shortwave static.

The first present I opened that Christmas morning was the cardboard box. Inside were twenty-four jars of grape jelly, each jar in its own waxy brown cell, a gift from one of my father's friends.

Oh, monstrous betrayal! "You told me it was a shortwave radio," I howled.

"I told you it was jelly," my father said. "You said it was a shortwave radio."

The jelly radio taught me the power of anticipation and desire. I'm certain that if I'd wished for a half-hour longer my incredible mental energy would have turned sugar into circuitry.

In the sensory carousel of Christmas recollections, there is the smell of the tires on my first bicycle and the cool touch of sharp metal girders lifted from a red, tin Erector Set box.

Close my eyes and I see the inside of Wellan's Department Store, hear the whoosh of brass message cylinders hurtling through pneumatic tubes, smell new merchandise carried on the arctic zephyrs of conditioned air, hear the babble of customers and clerks and the ding-ding of elevator doors opening.

Cars passing in the December street a few yards from my pillow call to mind the Christmas Eve I sneaked into the living room to fight sleep by counting the infrequent cars that passed our house. I was waiting for my mother to come home from her job in ladies' foundation garments.

Finally, there was the sound of her key in the lock and the sudden smell of her in the living room. When she finished fussing about my being up so late, I made her tell about the Christmas Eve that Louie Wellan found her crying at the foundation garments counter.

"I've told you that story before," she said.

"Tell it, again."

"It was late Christmas Eve. The store was closing. Everyone was putting on coats and hats and wishing people Merry Christmas. Some of the clerks were having a drink in the stockroom, but your presents and your sister's were in layaway. When I looked in my purse, the little envelope with my pay was gone. I looked under the counter, on the floor, in the wastepaper basket. All I could think was that someone had stolen it."

"I was sitting on a stool with my elbows on the counter crying when Mr. Wellan walked up."

Sometimes, it was Mr. Wellan and sometimes it was Louie Wellan. But always there was respect in my mother's voice when she said the name of the store's owner.

When my mother told a Louie Wellan story, she became a short, stout, elderly, Southern Jewish man. When I heard movie mogul Samuel Goldwyn speaking in a newsreel, I was shocked. He sounded like my mother telling a Louie Wellan story.

My mother loved Mr. Wellan. She told me that if I ever heard anyone saying mean things about Jews to think of him and the second pay envelope he didn't have to give her that Christmas Eve.

"He didn't know the money was stolen," my mother would say. "For all he knew, I'd made up the story."

That's the way that Louie Wellan story always ended.

What else? I remember a book called *Dragon Run* that I got the Christmas I was fourteen. *Dragon Run* was a mystery book written for serious readers. The Hardy Boys, even *The Shortwave Mystery*, held little for me after *Dragon Run*. Between that Christmas and the next, my mother died. In most ways that mattered, childhood was over.

If we had walked longer, I might have asked Mary if she thought Christmas memories, happy or sad, sustain us as adults. Does anticipation diminish with age or only the belief that anticipation will amount to anything?

But our walked ended. Mary had to dress for a party. Charged from the walk, I was eager to try to coax memory into words and paragraphs. A cool wind at my back, I headed home to write.

Lying warm in my bed tonight, I will hear the branches of an old yew tree squeaking against the window glass. In the morning, anyone who cares to look will see a man in his fifties walk out my front door, climb into a faded blue pickup truck, and drive off. But tonight, I, a child of no age on the verge of sleep, will lie warm beneath cold-clouded, December windows. In that briefest interval between consciousness and sleep, I may hear through the crackle of shortwave radio all my Christmases calling, calling, calling.